Eagle Eye

Eagle Eye

The Original Man of America, An Autobiography by
Robert Banks Cornelius, Jr., Narrated to and co-
authored by Professor Darnell A. Morehand-Olufade

Robert Banks Cornelius Jr. and Darnell A. Morehand-Olufade

ISBN-13: **9780692998571**
ISBN-10: **0692998578**
Library of Congress Registration Number: **TXu 2-066-578**
Library of Congress Control Number: **2017919154**
Darnell A. Morehand-Olufade, Wilton, CT
BISAC: **Biography & Autobiography / Artists, Architects, Photographers,
Biography & Autobiography / Personal Memoirs**

Dedication

I dedicate my autobiography to my Blackburn, Hudson, Banks, Cornelius, Ashley, and Peck families.

Acknowledgements

MY COUSINS, REVEREND Vivian Thomas-Breitfeld and Elaine Collins, for starting to trace the family history over thirty years ago and continuing to send copies of documents throughout the many years pertaining to the Blackburn, Hudson, Banks, Thomas, Stephens, and Cornelius families. Margie Shinholster, my cousin, who was born and raised in Dry Branch, Twiggs County, Georgia. Thanks be to the Creator for them. Pat Nixon and Emily, Lisabeth Hanson and her husband at the Family History Center, Church of Latter Day Saints, Manhattan, New York. A professor at Columbia University who encouraged me to do my artwork at The Art Students' League of New York and to research my family history at the Mormon Church, also known as The Church of Latter Day Saints. Peggy Fontenot, who was the photographer I met in Washington, DC, in September 2004 at the opening ceremony of the National Museum of the American Indian. She took what became a worldwide famous photo of me that I have chosen as the front cover of my autobiography. The late Reverend "Ike" (also known as Frederick J. Eikerenkoetter II) of the United Palace, New York City, who inspired me to do what I want to do, obtain what I want to have, and most of all BELIEVE IN MYSELF. Professor Darnell A. Morehand-Olufade, who suggested I write my autobiography, who traveled with me five times between the years 2013–2017 to Atlanta and Dry Branch Twiggs County, Georgia, to meet and interview my family members and take photos; typed the manuscript of my autobiography; and researched the Blackburn family at the New Echota Cherokee Capital Historical Site, Calhoun, Georgia, and Macon Georgia Family History Center Genealogy, Macon, Georgia.

About the Authors

I MET PROFESSOR Darnell A. Morehand-Olufade at the Leona Mitchell Southern Heights Heritage Center and Museum, Enid, Oklahoma, where my cousin Angela Molette is the curator of our cousin Leona Mitchell's museum. We were invited to attend the annual powwow, which is a Native American cultural celebration of family and friends of all tribal groups that come to participate in the event. I drove from New York City with some friends, and Professor Morehand-Olufade flew in from Phoenix, Arizona, where she worked as a student affairs administrator and a faculty associate and taught Ethnic Studies at Arizona State University, West Campus. We had never met before or heard of each other. I was already a retired carpenter who spent most of the time creating different Native American oil paintings and sculptures. The day that I arrived in Enid, I donated several of my paintings to the Leona Mitchell Southern Heights Heritage Center and Museum and participated in the powwow "Grand Entry" ceremony.

The Leona Mitchell Southern Heights Heritage Center and Museum is located at the end of the "Trail of Tears" in Enid, Oklahoma. I and my cousin Angela Molette try to keep the Native American traditions going because we are the descendants of those who suffered on the trail that started from New Echota Cherokee Capital (1825–1838), Calhoun, Georgia, and onto the designated areas of Indian Territory Oklahoma. The museum displays the recorded history of the Muscogee, Poarch Creek, Cherokee, Choctaw, Chickasaw, and Seminole Indians, who were also known as the "Five Civilized Tribes" before and after the Trail of Tears (early 1830s–1838). Angela Molette's parents' ancestral heritage is

Choctaw and Chickasaw. It was during a discussion between Professor Morehand-Olufade and me that I learned she taught African American History at Glendale Community College, Glendale, Arizona (2002–2009) and the Principles of Ethnic Studies at Arizona State University, West Campus, Glendale, Arizona (2007–2008). Her historical research focus is on lack Indians, and I informed her most Native Americans who are dark skinned do not refer to themselves as African American or Black, but as the indigenous peoples of "Turtle Island." As we became friends, we continued our discussions about the history of the Native American Nations, especially along the northeastern and southeastern coastlines of America.

In October 2008 I invited Professor Morehand-Olufade to meet with and interview Native Americans at the Shinnecock Reservation powwow in Southampton, Long Island, New York. She was amazed to see dark-skinned Indians, and this inspired her to write a book about me, the first dark-skinned Native American she ever met. In October 2009 she moved to Binghamton, New York, where she taught American History at Broome Community College, Binghamton, New York (2010–2012). Professor Morehand-Olufade moved to Wilton, Connecticut, and was hired as an adjunct professor (2014–present) to teach African American History I and II and American History I and II at the University of Bridgeport, Bridgeport, Connecticut. This gave her greater opportunities to attend the Shinnecock, Unkechaug, and Narragansett powwows and meet/interview Native American participants from 2010 to the present time. I introduced the professor to an entirely different world that very few people know about and the fact that there are Indians who come dark complexioned and are not mixed with any African ancestry.

---— ⚭ —---

Preface

I CHOSE TO write my autobiography after I had done very intense and thorough genealogical research about the ancestors of my father, Robert Banks Cornelius Sr. It was a surprise to me that they originated from London, England, as far back as the latter fifteen hundred. I became even more interested when my paternal ancestral line was so involved with the early colonial history of America from the sixteen hundred in Henrico County, Virginia, onto the eighteen hundreds in Greenville, South Carolina, and Houston County and Twiggs County, Georgia. My genealogy research confirmed the facts that my paternal ancestral roots are White, Native American, and Black. Professor Morehand-Olufade had extensive knowledge and experience in family history research as a former member of the Black Family Genealogy and History Society, Phoenix, Arizona (2006–2009). She understood my desire to know my family's roots and "who I am."

I know those who read my autobiography will gain the knowledge that Native Americans are of different complexions, from dark to light skin. In movies and television shows of the past, white men and women were deliberately chosen and dressed up to portray what an Indian looked like. In my autobiography I will prove it is not a myth, and it is true that Native Americans were and still are dark-skinned peoples. All you have to do is come to the Poospatuck Reservation (of the Unkechaug Nation) in Mastic, New York, and the Shinnecock Reservation in Southampton, Long Island, New York, and that will answer all the questions you have about dark-skinned Native Americans.

Table of Contents

My Life in Atlanta Georgia

—— ❦ ——

I WAS BORN in Atlanta, Georgia, on December 16, 1940, at a place called Summerhill on a street called Frazier. My father was Robert Banks Sr., born in Twiggs County, Georgia, outside of Macon. My mother, Gladys (née Nash) Banks, was born in Sandersville, Georgia. My parents met in the 1930s in Atlanta, where they married and settled. During that time they had two children. My sister Gladys was the first daughter, and I was the first son. When I was two years old, we moved from Summerhill to a place called Fifth Ward: the projects. My senior sister and I were born in my grandmother's house in Summerhill, and our siblings were born in the projects. My mother told me I was born with a veil over my eyes (also known as a caul), which meant I was born with the gifts of healing, spiritual insights, psychic abilities, and luck throughout my life.

I was three or four years old by the time I was aware of who I was, whereby I knew my Native American spirit. I had an uncle by the name of Lawrence who passed away when I was an infant. My mother told me he loved me so much that he would come and see me most every other day. He was a tall red man with freckles on his face, and he was my mother's oldest sister's husband. One day he told my mother he was coming back, but he died from the dust he inhaled as a construction worker. *2 No Good work opportunities*

But sure enough, he did come back in spirit. While washing dishes one day, my mother saw me lifted up in the air, and she knew it was my uncle Lawrence who had come back to see me. She got scared and went to the neighbor next door because she was too frightened to stay with me. When she came back into the house, she knew exactly when Uncle

1

Lawrence left because I was sitting on the floor smiling at him going out the door. After that I saw Uncle Lawrence every night. I saw him and could feel him. Sometimes he dressed in all white and sometimes in jeans. I was a little afraid because I knew it was not my mother or father. It was some type of spirit because Uncle Lawrence would be laughing as he stood over me. At that time, I had another sister, Virginia, and she and I slept at the top of the one big bed in our room, and my older sister, Gladys, slept at the bottom. They never saw Uncle Lawrence's spirit but me, even though they were all in the room with me. As I was going on ten years old, he quit visiting me. But I do feel his spiritual presence even to this day, and I think my ideas come from him. Uncle Lawrence was highly skilled— he could build anything—and very intelligent. I am quite sure I got my artistic abilities from him, even though he was not my blood relative. My artistic skills, such as drawing, became more prominent—that is, every day it showed as I took a pad and pencil and drew different-looking creatures: Superman, Batman and Robin, Dick Tracy, Donald Duck, Mickey Mouse, and all the cartoons in the funny papers.

I remember that you had to be six years old before you could go to school. I always felt much older than I was. A white couple had an old mule and a horse and buggy, and they sold apples at the projects. When they came by our house, I asked if I could help them, and they said yes. I was four years old. They would give me two baskets full of apples, and I would sell each basket containing about fifteen apples for ten cents. The women thought I was the cutest little black boy with the cutest little head, and they loved my complexion, which was pretty and smooth. They would buy apples from me because of the way I looked. I would sell the apples as fast as the old couple would hand the baskets to me. I sold all their apples in a day, and they would give me twenty cents at the end of the day. I thought it was a lot of money because you could buy quite a bit with it at that time, such as strap candy (different candies in a big bag) for an old Buffalo nickel with the Indian head on it. I would have about a dollar at the end of the week and about five or ten dollars at the end of the month.

I would save my money in a large jar and hide it in an upstairs closet in the bedroom. No one knew my money jar was hidden there. But one day my father found my money jar and took my entire thirty dollars in savings for carfare to go to work as a butcher. He promised he would pay me back at the end of the week. Instead, he gave me ten cents and then told me to give the ten cents back.

I remember when I was a kid my mother would be sitting on the porch with her long horsehair. I noticed she was different from the other women in the projects. During that time, I really didn't know I was a Native American, but I felt the power about myself and knew there was something different about my mother, my family, and me. I did mostly everything that a Native American person would do, and I was so different from the other kids. During this time my mother would never tell me who I was, even though she knew the background. I believe she thought I was not ready to receive at age six or seven the knowledge about my family background or that I could understand it. What she did not realize was that I was ready to know all my peoples and their Native American connection. I really think she did not want to tell me because I was riding my bike, skating, playing cowboys and Indians, and flying kites with my friends. I don't think she wanted to disturb my childhood, and she figured it would interfere with my Christmas, Thanksgiving, and Easter with the kids. She did not know I had an open spirit and was open to everything and ready to learn about my Native background. My mother always looked at me as one of her "special" children.

My father always wondered why I was different from him and my siblings. He treated me like he could not understand why I was so different. For example, I preferred to eat different foods. I would not want the Jell-O mixed with fruit cocktail everybody else was eating. My mother knew that I was a different child. She never said anything about her other kids being intelligent like she said about me. She did not care what my father said; she knew I was a special child. I could tell she favored me more than any of her other kids, and my sisters noticed this also. Even today, although I am a thousand miles away, she is still the same. I could

3

ROBERT BANKS CORNELIUS JR MOTHER, MRS. GLADYS
CORNELIUS, ATLANTA, GEORGIA 1960

never really figure out why my mother favored me over her other kids. I
think one day I am going to ask her, as I have not yet asked what it is she
favors in me over the rest of us. My brother and sisters can take a walk and
never come back as long as she has me around; she would never miss any
one of them. When I left Atlanta at sixteen, my mother seemed happy,
but I could sense she was not happy about my coming to New York.

By September 1945, a playmate of mine named Ben Jr. started school
because he was a year older than me. I thought we were the same age
because we played together, but my mother tried to explain to me that
he was older. I did not want to hear this, and I cried that I could not go to
school. By September 1946, I was ready to go to school, and I was happy.
My mother took me on the first day, and my father took me on the second
day. The name of the school was David Street School, and it is now known
as Mary M. Bethune Elementary School. On the third day of school, I

woke up and my parents went to work, so I was on my own to walk to school. An elderly woman named Miss Mitchell always wore a rag around her head and an apron; she looked something like Aunt Jemima (she was a very dark-skinned woman) and was very nice. She took care of my sister Virginia because my older sister, Gladys, and I went to school. On my way to David Street School, I had to cross what appeared to be a large highway. I believe my parents regarded me as an old spirit and never treated me like a little boy. They were not afraid about me crossing the highway or going anywhere in the neighborhood. My mother told me I always knew how to handle myself, and I was never up under my mother from the time I was a toddler. She enjoyed my siblings as young children but not me because I was always out and about doing things from two years old on. When I was four years old, I had several older acquaintances, including thirteen- and fifteen-year-old boys.

I had an uncle by the name of John Banks who had a dry-cleaning business right by my school, and I would stop to see him when I needed money. He would give me a nickel so that I could buy strap candy. I remember that as a student in the first grade, I read at a fifth-grade level. My teacher's name was Mrs. Whitehead, and her daughter, Jean, was in my class. I used to beat her daughter in the spelling contest, and she did not like that. Before coming to school each day, I would pick up my girlfriend, Marion. She was a pretty Native-looking girl with nice brown skin. I can still hear her mother saying, "Marion, here come your boyfriend. He come to pick you up for y'all to go to school together." When we got to the school one day, a teacher asked me if Marion was my sister because we always ate and played together and came and left school together. I wanted to tell the teacher that Marian was my girlfriend, but I didn't. Every day I would play in Marian's backyard after school for about an hour and then go home. My parents were never concerned about how long I was gone or where I was, and they never asked where I was. They had trust and faith in me, and I did nothing wrong. I was always playing.

We had a May Day play, and I wanted Marian to be my partner. Mrs. Whitehead chose a light-skinned girl named Jean to be my partner, and

I did not like this because I wanted pretty dark-brown Marian to be my partner. Mrs. Whitehead was bent on breaking up my young relationship with Marian. Mrs. Whitehead eventually got me out of the school with the excuse that it was too far for me to walk to. Thus, I attended Gray Street School for second grade, which was on the compound of the projects where I lived. At Gray Street School, I met a new girlfriend named Jessie Robinson; we were seven years old. Jessie and I were really tight, just like I was with Marian. When I got into the fourth grade, I attended E. P. Johnson Elementary School in Summerhill, where I was born. At this school and thereafter, I never had a female attachment like with Marian and Jessie. Eventually I went back to the Summerhill area to live with my maternal grandmother, Fannie Nash.

Before I went to Summerhill, I use to fight kids every day who passed my house in the projects. I became notorious in the area as a badass fighter. A high school kid named Billy started chasing me every day, but he never caught me. He probably wanted to teach me a lesson for beating up my peers who were afraid of me and had to pass my house. Everybody in the projects talked about how bad I was. My parents argued about this matter. My mother did not want me to be scared of anyone, but my dad did not like that I was always cutting up and beating up the kids. Miss Claudette, a neighbor who was really pretty, slightly heavy, and had a lovely brown complexion, called me a little badass and threatened to tell my father. Everybody said I was very strong as a little boy and such a badass, although I never thought I was bad. When one of my peers named Bobby, who lived on Bush Street across from the projects, would go to the store, he made sure to walk around the projects to avoid passing my house so that I would not see him and beat him up. Ms. Julia, who lived in the projects, liked me as a small child of seven or eight years old and called me Preacher. She said I had a cute little head. All the very pretty girls in elementary school liked me, perhaps because I was so rough or because I was called Preacher and they saw something different in me. Some of these girls had the Indian look, and others were high yellow with straight Indian-like hair. I think it was spiteful when my former teacher,

Bad Quality of Schooling,

Mrs. Whitehead, became jealous because I was smarter than her daughter and had me placed into the middle of the projects' elementary school where I learned *nothing*, the children were dumb, and I was always busy fighting. I refused to pick up a book and did not want to learn any more. Instead, I would draw. The teacher knew I was showing up her daughter, Jean, and her mean-spiritedness impacted my life academically forever. I became interested in art because I lost my book knowledge. I will always remember a writer said, "Who is smart? Everybody can do something the next person can't do. Hence, nobody is smarter than the other." We all have different gifts and utilize what we've got.

I was in the fifth grade when my elder sister and I stayed with Granny Nash. Gladys got pregnant in the ninth grade with her first daughter, Yvonne, also called Bump Bump, and my parents kicked her out. It was when I was staying with my grandmother that I first heard our family was Native American and *not* like the African Americans. My grandmother's father wore two long braids and a part in the middle of his head and would sit on the porch carving from wood. He had a dark complexion and was a very mean man. She finally left home in her teens and never contacted him again. I always felt I was Native American spiritually, and I would make arrows with a bird feather at the end and use string to wrap it to hold. I had a dream while a grown man living in New York that Granny Nash came to me and told me her people are Sioux. I questioned my grandmother about how we could be Native American when our skin color is black, and she said, "That don't mean nothing. You is Indian." More and more, white people were playing the roles of Indians on TV and in the movies, so I thought that all Indians were fair skinned. I also thought my grandmother was trying to make us something we were not. Now I know light-skinned Indians were mixed with the white race, thus resulting in their fair skin, which is not a true example of a natural-born Native American. I told my grandmother the other kids were the same color as we were, and she told me we were Indians and they were not, even though our complexions were the same. The Banks and Hudson which are the names of our families, were Montauk and Shinnecock Indians.

My first cousin Bobby was already living with my grandmother Nash, and he was two years older than me. He never had the Indian factor like me and was not going through the motions of being an Indian. I left Granny Nash when I was twelve years old and starting eighth grade at Booker T. Washington High School. I returned to live with my parents, who had a little shotgun-looking house on Paine Avenue. All the children slept in the same bedroom, and my brother and I slept in the same bed. Our bedroom was connected to the kitchen and bathroom. By this time there were eight of us (six girls and two boys), and so the house was very full. It was at this house where I started a bonfire in the backyard and made a bow and arrow. When Brenda, one of my twin sisters, came out of the house, I pointed the bow and arrow right at her. The arrow struck her on the cheek under her left eye, and she still bears the mark to this day. My siblings acted like regular little kids. I did not and was always more advanced and out there making money on my own. I was very different from my younger brother and sisters. We seldom played together because I lived with my grandmother, and during that time my mother had my twin sisters Wanda and Brenda. My brother, Rayfield, and I did not go to school together and had nothing in common. He was very much a mother's child and even so until today. I was close to my sister Virginia because she was nineteen months younger than me. We went to Turner, Archer, and Carver High Schools together. To be honest my sister Virginia would follow me everywhere I went and learned more from me than from our older sister, Gladys. I was never up any of my sisters that much and was more with my maternal grandmother than my own mother. One thing I remember: as children we would go to friends' birthday parties and did not like to eat cake, ice cream, or candies. It was strange to most people, but we just were not sweets-eating kids. We attended the birthday parties to play. I started eating sweets when I reached forty years old.

After this I started changing high schools every year. I never graduated from high school in Atlanta. I quit and came to New York at the age of sixteen. I attended the Church of Resurrection High School at the age of eighteen or nineteen and had an excellent math teacher who was about twenty-three years old and blind. I quit this school in the twelfth grade and never went back to finish. I liked school, but they never taught art, and if they had, it would probably have helped me to finish. At the E. P. Johnson Elementary School in the sixth grade, Mrs. Banks (I am quite sure she was related to me, but I did not know it, as my last name is Cornelius) had an art class, and I enjoyed art. She would tell the kids I would become a great artist someday. She took a keen interest in my drawings of Tonto, the Lone Ranger, the Green Hornet, and Bugs Bunny, and she showed me how to sketch really fast. I was a born artist, and another guy named Horace and I were the best in the class. My first cousin Bobby, Horace, his brother, and I used to sit in my grandmother's house and draw for hours as a form of play. Of course, I was born with the gift of drawing and still have it today.

The street my grandmother lived on was Conway Place, and the house sat on four pillars. We would go under the house for coal to burn in the potbelly stoves that we used to cook food and keep warm. With no electricity, a large kerosene lamp lit the one-bedroom home. Bobby and I slept with Granny. My aunt the preacher, Annie Ruth Ross, my mother's sister, also lived in the house. Because she was a preacher, we went to church Monday, Wednesday, and Friday and three times every Sunday; we never missed a Sunday. It was an old sanctified churched called the Church of God on Marden Street in Summerhill. The older church is now a landmark next to the new, larger church. My name is in a little black book the size of a telephone book that shows Bobby and me as young members of the church.

As an innocent young child going to the Church of God with everyone in the household, I thought I would actually see God. I kept asking Bobby if we would see God, and he said, "Yes, there is his hat hanging up there." Then a great big old black preacher, Brother Wilson, came into the room and took up his hat, and Bobby said, "There he is." I said, "That ain't God," and Bobby said, "That is the only one you gonna ever see, my man." The older men who played marbles with Bobby nicknamed him

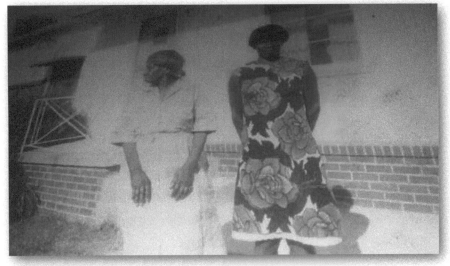

LEFT: MRS. GLADYS NASH (GRANNY) AND HER DAUGHTER MRS.
GLADYS CORNELIUS, ATLANTA, GEORGIA – AUGUST 1961

Haircut. Bobby was two years older than me and much shorter, but no one ever asked which of us was older, as most people thought we were brothers. We were first cousins: his mother, Carrie, was my mother's junior sister. She was not a religious person by any means. Bobby was born in New York, but his mother brought him to Atlanta at the age of four. Bobby did not like New York as a child, and that is why his mother brought him to her mother, Granny Nash, in Atlanta. My grandmother used to tell me blacks, Jews, and Natives ran the world, and then the white people mixed with us, rewrote our history, hijacked our cultures, and hid everything from us to make us feel we were nothing.

I ended up staying with my grandmother because I wanted to follow my sister Gladys. I was very close to my elder sister and always wanted to be near her. My granny Nash was very spiritual, and this was when I first learned about our Native American roots. I had always felt different from others and proud of myself. During recess in elementary school, I would dig in the red clay of Atlanta and build teepees and adobe houses while the other children were busy fighting. The teachers always thought I was slow when I went to my new school, E. P. Johnson in Summerhill, but they didn't know my peaceful and spiritual grandmother influenced me. I had already acted bad and fast while living in the projects at Fifth Ward on the other side of town.

All the boys in this class were killed in their twenties right there in Summerhill. Sugar and I once fought because his girlfriend claimed I was cursing her, and Sugar confronted me about it. Sugar knew I was not scared of him or anybody else in the school. Sugar beat me up first, and when I came back the next day, I beat the crap out of him, even though he did not want to fight me a second time. I came at Sugar with such a vengeance because his girlfriend lied on me, and I was determined to prove that I could fight better than him. Another student, Charles Heard, had warned Sugar about me. Charles had lived in the Fifth Ward on the other side of town and knew about my reputation as a hard and strong fighter. When Sugar saw me, he commented on my height and how I had filled out with a broad chest. Sugar appeared not to have grown from the time we were in elementary school. This was the last fight I had at E. P. Johnson Elementary School.

At E. P. Johnson, we learned math, science, English, reading, writing, and art. My academic ability was shot as I lost interest in doing schoolwork. Instead, I would do nothing but draw as my homework. From this time on, I felt it was not important for my life to learn all those subjects, and I still feel the same. I used to always tell my father I never had homework, and I refused to do it. My drawing was very significant, and I always felt God would take care of me, even without the book smarts I had lost when I went to school in the projects. I wanted to go to college and get a degree, but with my grandmother telling me about the Creator, I knew I would be taken care of. I never did lack for anything in my life.

I attended Booker T. Washington High School off Martin Luther King Drive, which used to be named Henry Street. I was thirteen years old when I attended for one year. The next year I entered Turner High School. The following year I went to Archer High School and after that to Carver Vocational School, where I learned bricklaying at the age of fifteen going on sixteen.

TOP PHOTO: DAVID STREET ELEMENTAR SCHOOL. BOTTOM PHOTO: ROBERT
BANKS CORNELIUS JR.
STANDING NEXT TO BOOKER T. WASHINGTON STATUTE, BOOKER T.
WASHINGTON HIGH SCHOOL, ATLANTA, GEORGIA, MAY 2012

I did not like any of these schools, but despite my failing to retrieve my
early book smarts, the Creator carried me through. None of the schools
could give me what I was looking for. At the age of seventy, I now realize
the Creator was with me always, no matter what I chose to do. Before I
came to New York, I was working with my eldest sister at Pete Country
Club in Atlanta, Georgia where white people went to eat lunch and dinner. My sister worked in the daytime, and I would work in the evening
after she went to her apartment. It was a very rich and aristocratic place,
with tennis courts, a golf course, and a swimming pool. I started washing
dishes and eventually I waited tables. Gladys had been working there for

about two years, and I made a lot of money through tips. I was twelve years old, and after I started waiting tables, I saved my money. I started thinking about buying a car. I bought a 1940 Chevrolet and paid $109 cash. I had no license, but I knew how to drive. Nobody ever had a car in my immediate family, and I was the first one. My whole family was so proud of me. The reason why I bought it is because I always saw the other guys' fathers had cars, and my father did not have one. I figured he would eventually get one when he saw that I had bought one. My father did buy a car later that year.

NEWLY BUILT OLD MARION BAPTIST CHURCH, DRY BRANCH, TWIGGS COUNTY, GEORGIA.
ROBERT BANKS CORNELIUS JR. 12 YEARS OLD, ATLANTA, GEORGIA

I used to put my money up in the attic, and eventually my father and sister Virginia took my money without asking me. Virginia would buy perfume and cosmetics with my money and wear my nice sweaters, complete with her lipstick marks and perfume, to high school. Virginia was buying her school friends lunch every day with my money. She used to see our father go into the attic and take my money constantly. I never knew they were taking money I had saved from working at the county club.

I had a bad experience with my car when I went into a drive-in restaurant called the Rainbow and backed into Jimmy the manager's car. As I went to pull out, my brakes lost all their brake fluid, and I could not stop. Jimmy came out all excited, shouting, "You hit my car! You hit my car!" As a young man, I was not excited at all, even though I had no driver's license. I asked Mr. Jimmy how much it was to get another chrome, and he told me fifty-eight dollars. Then the police came and made me take driving classes, which I did for about a week. I don't even remember paying Jimmy his money. Next, I parked the car in my mother's driveway on Paines Avenue, where it stayed for about one year. One of my father's colleagues saw the car and asked me if I wanted to sell it. I said yes because I did not know all it needed was some brake fluid, and I could have been driving it. He asked me how much I wanted for it, and I told him twenty-five dollars. He did not have the money then but came back that Friday with cash. Boy, I was glad to get the money because the car was just sitting there, as I thought something serious was wrong with it. I wanted him to hurry and give me the twenty-five dollars because I thought I was getting over on him and the car was really damaged. But guess what? You want to hear something cute? After he gave me the money, he told me all it needed was brake fluid. He actually got over on me because I thought it needed a new motor. This was only one mistake.

I met the most influential people in my life when I was about twelve years old and living in Atlanta. I heard about Elijah Muhammad, an albino with a star and crystal red-and-white ring on his finger (like a half-moon). That he was albino and wore the ring got my attention. He told me to follow him to where I could hear some of Muhammad's teachings. I went to a place called Auburn Avenue in Atlanta, Georgia, to a little store-front that had the US flag on one side and the star and crescent flag on the other side. The albino was the teacher. He pointed a long stick at the blackboard and shook his head. He told us there were two worlds in America. The most fascinating thing was it seemed like the Islamic teachings fitted me better than the Christian teachings. What he was telling us was something it seemed I had already been taught in another life, but I had lost the knowledge. The teaching of Islam was familiar to me, but in the present life, Christianity just wasn't for me. I remember that, as a kid, I was particular about what I ate. The minute he said we don't eat swine, it struck me that he was right and that I was forced to eat something I was not used to. He was about the only person I was interested in and could relate to before I left Atlanta.

Move to New York City to Start a New Life and Learn Professional Skills

———————— ɋ ————————

I STAYED IN Atlanta for a while, and then one day, I decided to go to New York by Greyhound bus. I really did not want to leave home, as I had never been to New York or anywhere else outside of Atlanta. I thought my mother and father would hate for me to go, but instead, they helped me out the door and wished me the best. I was given my mom's baby sister's address: 144th Street between Lenox Avenue and Seventh Avenue, Harlem, New York. When I got off the Greyhound bus at the Port Authority, everybody looked very much like gangsters, wearing dark shades and moving fast. I never saw people move so quickly. I also never saw so many different ethnicities or nationalities; it was frightening to me coming out of the Atlanta setting with only our two main races. You can imagine what this situation was like coming out of the Deep South in 1956. I had $2,000 cash with me. My small suitcase contained ten brand-new white shirts, neckties, three pairs of slacks, and two or three pairs of shoes. I traveled light because I planned to stay only a couple of weeks and then return to Atlanta.

It was a shock to see so much garbage on the streets of New York city and people throwing garbage out the window or into the backyard. Whiskey bottles and beer cans were thrown out the windows at night, clinking on the pavement. Here I was coming from pretty green Atlanta and seeing this horrible scene of garbage everywhere on the streets of Harlem. My mother gave the address of her baby sister, Carrie, so I would have a place to rest my head, as I had never left home before and was only sixteen years old. This was the sister who used come to Atlanta and brag about how beautiful New York was and painted pictures that New York had golden streets. She lived at 144th Street, apartment 6-D, on the top floor with no elevator. I said to myself, "I know my aunt does not live in this mess," but what a shock it was to me when she opened the door. I just knew she did not stay in that dump the way she used to brag about New York when she came to Atlanta. I will never forget she told me to never let anybody in the door, and I was scared to even go to the door. One day the doorbell rang, and a really pretty girl insisted I let her in. She begged me to let her in because she was a Jehovah's Witness like my aunt and wanted to talk to me about the Watchtower. She was by herself, although Jehovah's Witnesses usually come in groups. I continued to talk to her through the closed door, refusing to open it. Through the peephole, I could see she wore glasses and looked like a college girl. She vowed not to bite me, but my aunt had put the fear in me not to let any man or woman into her house.

While my aunt and her husband were working, I would walk up and down Lenox Avenue with the spare key my aunt gave to me. About a month after my arrival, I ran into one of my young schoolmates from Atlanta sitting in a Chinese restaurant and wearing dark shades. He had tried to get me to come to New York six months earlier. We continued our friendship and became hustlers, playing numbers, shooting craps, and the like. My aunt was not charging me rent, and of course, and I had my $2,000, which lasted me two years. I got a kitchenette on 127th Street between Fifth and Seventh Avenues, for eight dollars a week, and I stayed there for two years. I would eat at a Chinese restaurant (we called it the Japs) and get a big plate of rice, oxtail, and toast with a large glass of ice tea, and it cost one dollar and fifty cents. I ate this every day for a year. We did anything to keep from getting locked up and to make money. Before I came to New York, I never used my head—in other words, as Miss Ruth told me, I got smart and wise, became a carpenter and an artist, and went back to high school where I discovered I was good at math and science. I was never exposed to all this in Atlanta. Since leaving the South, I never spent more than three days in Atlanta whenever I went back. Before she died, my grandmother Nash said to me, "Ain't you glad you went to New York? It was the best thing you did to move to New York." To this day I don't like Atlanta. A street bum once said to me, "Man, you really don't like it down here in Atlanta," and I said, "No, I don't." He was right. I wish I had given him a dollar, as he read my mind correctly while I was pumping gas into my car. This short discussion I had with the bum was during one of my rare trips from New York City to see my family in Atlanta, Georgia.

My first real job was when my aunt got me to work construction with a man she knew and who was a Jehovah Witness. He lived around the corner and was named Tatum. He was a black man who looked white, and he was the foreman. My work was pulling nails out of two-by-fours and plywood. Tatum liked me a lot and called me Junior. I quit after a month because I was not a given an opportunity to do what he could do as a carpenter. Next, I started working in a restaurant washing dishes. I got my food for free. I also worked at the Hunter College cafeteria for two years while attending Twenty-Sixth Street Carpentry Apprentice School and when the campus moved from 26th Street and Lexington to Huston Street off Hudson Street downtown. I got into carpentry due to a Puerto Rican named Lucky. We both wanted to do proper carpentry, and he got us into the New York City District Council of Carpenters School before the statute of limitations to attend the school within a specified time. I got a certificate to become a licensed carpenter. I am presently in the union as a retiree. After this I took a four-year chaplaincy program and became a chaplain in the early 1990s. I worked at New York University Hospital and Bellevue Hospital, seeing patients and prisoners. The prisoners used to ask me to call their wives. One day I saw a prisoner on the street, and he questioned me seriously about not calling his wife. I could have worked in the prisons but was not interested in doing so, as it was like bringing my work home.

When I became a carpentry apprentice in 1977, I realized I came from a building family, as most of my maternal uncles (my dad's brothers) were also skilled builders or worked for General Motors in Detroit, Michigan. My father was a butcher for more than sixty years and retired in Atlanta as a foreman for the company White Division, which had an abattoir. I worked all over the five boroughs, as well as midtown Manhattan, on different sites. I built shelves and closets and put up drywall and ceilings after I did a room-by-room layout of the interior of apartments, houses, and big buildings—that is, the skyscrapers. I did this work for about ten years until I had a work-related accident. It happened at the Riverbank State Park on 125th and 145th Streets where they built the sewage plant to purify the water. I stepped on a nail, and it went through my left foot. I was rushed to the medical center on 168th Street and Broadway for treatment. I went out on workers' compensation and never returned to that type of work. As a union member doing carpentry, I was making forty dollars an hour. I took out my $13,000 pension around 1987 when I could not work again.

I worked as a laborer in 1980–1981 under an organization called Black Economic Survivor in the Bronx on Long Wood Avenue, and we would go around and fight for jobs. The blacks, Puerto Ricans, Native Americans, and any people of color had to actually fight to get jobs. Sometimes they would call the police on us, and some would get locked up. I was determined not to get locked up just to get a job. It did not make sense to me to get locked up for trying to work. I figured if I was to be locked up, it would be for robbing a bank, not trying to get a job. We used to ride on a yellow school bus from job site to job site, begging the foremen to hire one of us. We rode to construction sites all over Brooklyn, Staten Island, and the five boroughs looking for our colleagues. Some places would hire a few men, but some places would not. This was due to discrimination against all minorities. All races were on the buses but never a white boy.

I was lucky to meet the guy who headed the organization. He was Spanish, and his name was Lucky. There was a carpenter's school on Twenty-Sixth Street and Lexington Avenue between Lexington and Third. I realized I had the talent to do something else besides labor. I had a dream that I was a layout man. This means you take a plum bar and you go from the ceiling to the floor and make a straight line. You are able to divide up a large space into separate rooms, such as a living room and bedroom. After I told Lucky about my dream, he said he would get me into the carpenter's school, but he had only a week to do it. He gave me the papers to go down there right away. I had only three days to get the papers there. I had to wait about two months to be called. Otherwise, I would have waited five more years to get into the school.

This gift came from God because I saw it as plain as day in my dream about how to be a layout man. Not everyone has this gift, but Lucky realized where I should be and what type of work I should do. This is how I got into the carpenters' union. It is great to be able to build and be a carpenter but it's greater to get into the union. This is why you attend the school, as it is the only way to get into the union and get benefits. I went to carpenter's school for four years, achieved my license, and became a union member for life. On my card it reads, "Qualified Operator's License for Power Action Tool #66757 Safety and Speed." It's come in handy because I can put nails into the stubs and drive them into the concrete. It shoots like a gun—pow!—and goes into the concrete. It is a very important tool to have, and I still have it in my closet. My first real job coming out of the school was at the Riverbank State Park at 125th Street and the Hudson River. We were building a sewer and also connecting it with fresh water, all combined, that runs through the city of New York. I liked this job because it was interesting, and I found out how different things worked.

This was the first time I ever worked with West Indian peoples. I found out some were prejudiced against American blacks and some were not, as it depended on what islands they were from. The Jamaicans were prejudiced against me, but the Trinidadians were friendly with me. The Jamaicans did not want to show me anything and just were not that good. My wife is a Jamaican, and she wanted me to take her there so she could tell them off for me. I never did take her down to a construction site because she would have showed off and talked loud. She felt if they knew I was married to a Jamaican woman, they would not have messed with me. So you see, people of color are prejudiced against one another, according to where you come from. But if I had taken my Jamaican wife to them, they would have acted differently toward me. I thought I knew what prejudice was and that it went no further than black and white, until I came to New York and found out black people, according to where they

Prejudice + Discrimination
Still present.

20

are from, are prejudiced against American blacks too. This is why now I take everybody as an individual and according to their behavior. I don't give a shit what color you are.

My aunt Annie, the Pentecostal preacher, was also a psychic, and she told me when I was little that I was going to be important and do something special and big in life. In 1977, my aunt Ruby had a vision of me getting hit by a car. Sure enough, later that day, I was hit by a car around 9:00 p.m. and taken to the hospital with a compound fracture. I was in the hospital for six months. My friend who was with me ran straight, but I started climbing steps, and the car jumped the curb, ran up the steps, and struck me. While I was in the hospital, I could hear my aunt talking to me softly in my head: "I told you to be careful, and now you got hit." She saw the accident as if she was watching TV, and it was not a dream. I was about twenty-two or twenty-three years old and was on crutches for eight months after getting out of the hospital. Dr. Gary Gonza (an East Indian) was the orthopedic surgeon who put a solid-gold plate with his name written on it in my left leg. This held all the bone and muscle together, and if he had put cheap metal into my leg, I would have had more surgeries throughout the years as I got older. Now that I am seventy years old, I am still doing fine and have never had any problems.

I became a Mason around 1978–1979 with Lodge Timbuktu of King Solomon Hall, 125th Street between Madison and Fifth Avenue. Once a Mason, always a Mason. I joined because I felt my knowledge would increase if I became a Mason. My math, carpentry, art, painting, carving, sculpting, and poetry skills were enhanced, and reasoning with and understanding people made me a better person. I learned to maintain my temple, which is made up of the body, mind, and spirit, and not to be so quick-tempered with people. I realized people could say things and not know who they are saying it to. I learned to keep calm, to control my temper, and to keep out of trouble because I better understood life and people. Since I became a Mason, I am a much better person. When I first became a Mason, I was told everybody was going to bring forty-four pieces of chicken in a basket. I got there and realized I was the only one who bought the forty-four pieces of chicken from Kentucky Fried Chicken. Everyone said thank you very much and started laughing. They told me this was my first initiation into the Masons, as I also brought the rolls, the five liters of soda, and the cups with ice. I enjoyed being around my fellow Masons, and the initiation rites and teachings were beneficial to the lodge members and me.

I met Janice Smith in 1979, and she gave birth to my first son, Ohene Kwadwo Opoku Banks Cornelius. She had been married before to a serviceman who had been killed. She had a child from her previous marriage, a son name Omar. She lived off her husband's pension after the US government held up the monies for about twenty years after he died. She did get paid retroactively about two years ago. We were together about two years, but she chose to move out because I was too strict with her. She wanted freedom to get high every once in a while, and I would not stand for it. She was born and raised in New York City and used to sing in the choir. Janice passed away in 2017. She was very intelligent and pretty when she was young. We remained the best of friends because there was no animosity between us. We were closely connected because of our son, Kwadwo. She was aggressive with other people but always meek with me. Most people could not put us together, as I was so mild in temperament.

When I was able to go back to work, I became a carpenter. I also did freelance carpentry for a while and was always in the New York City District Council of Carpenters union on Hudson Street. I married a Jamaican woman, Carleen Ramsay, in 1986 in New York. She was born in Montego Bay, Jamaica, West Indies, around 1951–1952. She was a nurse's Aide who made up the hospital beds. I told her to go back to school, and with my encouragement, she attended a nursing school in Long Island. She became a registered nurse, and I drove her to school every day until she graduated. After that she started acting strangely, and then we broke up. She went to school on a study grant. I made sure she achieved her goals, but then she met someone else, and she did not want to make the marriage work. During our six years of marriage, we had one son named Ali-Rakman Raheem Cornelius. She lied to her family that I was a bad man and told her mother she could not stay in the house with me, as if I was beating her. I finally walked out of the marriage after being told to get out every day and after she lied on me.

When my sons were born, I was close to them throughout their lives. Both boys were good children who were never spanked. After I broke up with my wife, my younger son, Ali, never came around when he grew up because she talked against me. It was the opposite with my eldest son; his mother always told him to be close to and love his father. Ali's mother is a Seventh-Day Adventist and so is supposed to be religious, but she told him lies about me, and we are not close now that he is grown. Kwadwo, my oldest, graduated from Saint Lawrence University in 2004 with a degree in theater arts. Ali attended Borough of Manhattan Community College, majoring in graphic arts. I have one grandson named Jeremiah Banks Cornelius. He has a speech problem that is being corrected by attending a special school. I hope and pray to the ancestors that he will talk really well.

ROBERT BANKS CORNELIUS JR. (CENTER) WITH SONS ALI CORNELIUS (LEFT) AND KWADWO CORNELIUS (RIGHT): FAMILY THANKSGIVING DINNER - NOVEMBER 2014

I always traveled with my mother, but my father never took me anywhere or gave me money either. I first traveled to California in 1979 to see my sister Linda, and I met my mother there. We made arrangements to go to Las Vegas. Linda had an old car, and as we crossed the desert, she could not turn on the air-conditioning because the car would stop. It was terribly hot, and there were signs stating we should *not* turn on the car air-conditioning. When we got to Las Vegas, my sister and I lost all our money at the casino. We went over to our mother, who was playing the slot machines. She had been winning, but when we came to her, she started to lose. My mother told us to take "our broke asses" back over there where we came from, and when we left her, she started to win again. That same evening, we went back to Long Beach, California, and the drive was cooler. I could not get used to the hot days and cool nights of California or to the attitude of the police authority and the way it was set up. They would lock you up if you jaywalked and were from out of town, which is not a nice way of dealing with visitors.

I never liked California and did not care to do a return visit. On top of that, the people are very prejudiced, and I found out they are worse than those in Mississippi. I had a black female friend who was knocked down by the police because she jaywalked, and they beat her and took her to jail. She returned to New York and sued them in Los Angeles around 1968. They had treated her like she had robbed a bank. I do not like anything about California, be it Los Angeles or anywhere else. When she came back to New York, she showed me her cast and told me how they broke her arm. After that I knew I never want to live anywhere that is behind the times and that thinks black people's lives don't mean anything. I have seen more racism in New York and California than in Georgia. In Georgia, when the police came, you really had done something, and everybody in the neighborhood knew you had done it. In New York, the police just shoot your ass down as an innocent person—you would not even have to be a threat—and they would get away with it. And they can know you are not the one, and you would take the blame for it anyway. I thought that Mississippi, Alabama, and Georgia were prejudiced, but it ain't nothing like what goes on in New York, Chicago, and Detroit. And that doesn't count going to upstate New York, where they look at you like they've never seen a black face before and like you are a criminal, and they're ready to pull their guns to shoot you.

I can remember when my eldest son, Kwadwo, was going to Saint Lawrence University in Canton, New York. My girlfriend at that time was very light skinned. I know the police thought I was a Native American with a white girl, and they stopped us in the car ten feet from the university gate. I asked the police why they stopped me, and they said I made a U-turn about a mile away from the university. I asked them why they didn't stop me then, but he could not explain. He only spotted me when I got near the gate. I knew this because I didn't make a U-turn a mile back, and this was the first time I was ever stopped by the police in Canton. Until then, I'd never had a fair-skinned woman in the car when I visited the campus. I expected the policeman to give me a ticket, but all he wanted to see was what the woman I had in the car really looked like—that is, whether she was white or a light-skinned black woman. I know that in New York State, the white people still do not get what integration means. I'm not saying that nobody is trying to be integrated, but love does not know color or race. So you see, everybody should get used to different races of people mixing because even if you don't like it, you cannot stop it.

A lot of people have never seen a dark-skinned indigenous person, but you cannot stop my traditions, actions, or ways of eating. Don't worry about other people. Just worry about yourself, and everything will be fine. Instead of trying to find out who is what race and who is supposed to be with whom, you should focus on who you are. Those who worry about the race of other people should focus on who they are instead of spending time on who others are and worrying about where they are going. You see why I am writing this book, because everything in it is no bull but reality instead. I noticed rich people don't ever worry about color and races; it is always the poor people who keep up the bull. Once you stop worrying about color and race, you become rich mentally, financially, and of course, spiritually. So you see, I never care about color or race. I deal with the individual and don't give a damn what color or race the person is. This was not taught to me at home or school; it came directly to my inner being from the Great Spirit of the whole universe.

A mistake I made was when I was forty-six or forty-seven years old. I bought a beautiful burgundy Firebird with a big bird on the hood, bucket seats, and the gears on the floor. A guy put a brand-new motor in it, and when you turned it on, you barely heard the car. I was married at that time, and I got the car from an auction. My wife did not like the car from day one. She wanted me to get a van so that I could work for myself. When I came home from the auction in the Firebird, she was mad because I told her I was going to get a van. She did not want a car I could look good in. As a typical woman, she wanted me to drive something I could make money off of, as she was all about money, not looks. Eventually I got money to get a van for about $2,000 at auction. Guess what? It needed a damn motor. I had sold the Firebird for seventy-five dollars because I wanted to get rid of it so as not to pay insurance on both vehicles. So, I lost money buying the van when I went to Hunters Point and was charged $500 for a motor, and another guy charged $600 to put it in. After this I separated from my wife, and the van broke down again on McNeil Street in Long Island. The van stayed there, and I caught the Long Island Railway coming back and forth to New York City.

One day I was riding around with Chief Mayo and a guy had a Cadillac De Ville that he wanted $500 for. I bought this beautiful car, and it lasted me four months before it went up in smoke. The engine was no good, but I drove it around, spending money on it constantly. Next, I bought a Chevy Nova, which was in excellent shape. I never serviced it or put oil in it for about three years. A Nova taken care of properly could last forever, as they don't break down. The first time it broke down, I just gave it away. After that a married couple who worked for the New York paper told me they were giving me a car. It was a beautiful blue Cadillac with blue leather seats. He told me he owed money on tickets and would pay them off but that I should not change the title into my name or insure it right away. The minute he mentioned tickets, I did not want to lose the car, so I changed the title into my name. Guess what? I did not have the car but a week. I thought somebody had stolen it, and I went to the precinct. The cop checked the records and found my Cadillac had been pulled in under my name for outstanding tickets. I told him I never got any tickets. I went downtown and discovered the white van I had owned six years ago. I still owed $6,000 on it because the guy who was fixing it kept it on the street in front of his house. The judge told me not to pay it because in only three months the statute of limitations would run out.

I did not have $1,000 to get the blue Cadillac out of the impound where it was held for two days. They auctioned it for about $200. The guy who gave it to me was so upset because he told me he was going to pay his tickets, and I was to wait to put my name on the title. I almost lost the white van because I did not know I was getting all the tickets on it. The guy who was fixing it never did. Then a mechanic named Eli finally fixed it for me, and Ms. Nichols paid him $200. She kept the van in her driveway and stored old clothes in it for the church. This goes to show you one can make mistakes when young and also when much older. After all these car matters, I started working for Budget Rent a Car and could get a car on discount when I needed to travel. I live in the city and use public transportation, but I still would like to have a car to go to places outside of the city, such as Long Island, Washington, DC, Philadelphia, and others.

I am not like the average guy who rides up and down on the subway and who doesn't need a car. They don't need a car because they don't go anywhere. Eventually I will get some money for another car but not a brand-new one. My dream is a white Cadillac with red leather seats. If not that, then a burgundy Firebird with a big bird on the hood like I had before and should never have gotten rid of. I will be getting another car because I like to travel. I am a Sagittarius, and we like to travel, like highly educated things, and like to save money. We are fighters, but we are easy to be hurt. We are under the planet of Jupiter with the twelve moons. I used to teach a little astrology and can still teach it. But I have moved on to other things, like my sculptures and painting. Because I am a retired carpenter, once in a while people request that I put up shelves, build cabinets, and do light stuff to make some change. When I am not doing that,

I write poetry and create my artworks. But I cannot wait to get permission to do these sculptures for the park in Philadelphia and the reservation in New York. My goal is to go back to my grandmother's house in Twiggs County, Georgia, and to keep researching my grandmother's history so that I can pass it on to my kids and their kids. Then they can know where they come from. All the research I am doing is going into this book.

I traveled to Africa in 1982 with Bishop Bonner of the Refuge Temple on 124th Street and Seventh Avenue, Adam Clayton Powell Road, Harlem, New York. I was baptized in this church. I remember Mr. Fleming came after me to be baptized by Reverend George every Sunday at Antioch Baptist Church, Northside Drive, Atlanta, Georgia. I was about four years old and was frightened of Mr. Fleming, who had light-gray eyes. He told me he was going to get me and baptize me. I would hide behind my mother whenever he came toward me while I was playing on the porch at home. This is the church where my mother sent my older sister, Gladys, and me to attend Sunday school. Along with about fifty Refuge Temple congregational members, I flew to Monrovia, Liberia, and then onto Dakar, Senegal, for a week. We went to build a school in a Liberian village, but I stayed only a week in each area. The major thing I ate was rice and fish—that is, a big plate of rice without vegetables and a piece of fish. Some other tribes at the market ate true African food, such as green bananas, fish, yams, plantains, and cassava but not rice. When I went to Senegal, a reader, or psychic, said New York is the best place for me. New York is my town, not Atlanta, and coming here at sixteen was the best thing I could have done. What I liked about Africa is that they speak Mandingo, French, and Walla (their native language) and that black people speak other languages; it is inspiring to hear their voices when they speak proudly and with dignity. I liked Senegal because it is a Muslim country. It was cleaner, and the people were faster than those in Liberia.

Even though the cabbies try to cheat you of your money, I did not hold this against all the Africans. In Senegal, the people laughed at me when I spoke English. I must admit the French language sounds beautiful when the Senegalese talk to one another, dance, and sing. They are lovely-looking people who are graceful and poised in movement. Liberia

28

was different in that the people were friendlier, as it is a Christian country and they have their own culture. The country was dirtier than Senegal, which is a Muslim country. We were told the Senegalese would look down on us, and they would cheat me by overcharging the cab rides to the hotel, as they know foreigners have trouble calculating the French money. Dakar reminded me of New York, and everybody moved at a fast pace. The men wear white mostly, the people are tall and slender, the men are mostly black complexioned, and the women have fairer skin, brown to light brown. The Mandingoes are jet black and pretty. I saw no difference between New York and Dakar. There was a smell of wild animals in the atmosphere. I went to Gorée Island, Senegal, where the slaves were taken and kept in chains before they were put onto slave ships. I took a photo of the chains that are still on the walls, and I could imagine how the slaves felt coming across the Atlantic Ocean on the ships.

I and Bishop Bonner, went into the villages to observe how the people lived. I noticed they had different-shaped heads from tribe to tribe, and I asked why. This was so they could tell who came from which tribe. They shaped the babies' heads at birth. I saw a man who was from the Bassa tribe in Liberia go under the river water with the fish, and Chris, a native of the Bassa tribe, told me people live under the water and their houses are also under the water. The man never came back up, and this amazed me. I celebrated my fortieth birthday on December 16, 1980, by climbing up a coconut tree by the Atlantic Ocean in Liberia, shaking a bunch of coconuts down, and drinking the juice. Liberia is like a huge village. The houses were shacks and seemed like back in the old times. It was a good experience to be over in Africa and to learn about the African tribes. When I got back to America, I could not tell the difference between black Americans and Africans unless they spoke. When I came home, I cooked and ate a great big plate of rice, without vegetables, and a piece of fish, just like the people I saw in Liberia and Senegal. I was proud to have gone to Africa, and although it might be home to some of my ancestors, America is more my taste. I don't know where my ancestors come from in Africa, but I do have proof of who my Native American ancestors were. I have nothing against the Africans and wish I could find an African ances-tor. But one thing I do know is that the Africans were not the only dark-skinned peoples of the world. The Native peoples of America were also dark-skinned until the Europeans mixed with us. I am not going to say I am something I have no proof of, but I can prove I am a Native American. I would be glad to accept African ancestry if I can find proof.

I still eat African foods like fufu, yams, cassava, and everything Africans eat. I also eat everything the Native Americans eat, such as corn, fry bread, venison, buffalo, and a lot of seafood. I also like Italian food, including spaghetti, lasagna, and red wine. When I do my sculpture, I eat cheese and take a sip of wine, and I can work you under the table. I am crazy enough to do what the Italians do. Europeans eat a medium steak, potatoes, and salad. I tried but prefer my steak well done. I also watch the Jews and how they eat and enjoy kosher foods. I also like Chinese food and use chopsticks. At least two times a week, I eat rice and duck with chopsticks. So you see, we are real Native Americans who are not prejudiced against anybody or the way they eat and live.

I moved out to Long Island in 1992–1995 and did not like it because it would get so cold and the highways would freeze terribly. When I had to travel back and forth to New York City I carried hundreds of dollars in my wallet because when my car needed towing it would cost me nearly two hundred dollars to take it to a garage for repairs. After this I bought a twelve-passenger white van and carried Muslim kids from Clara Muhammad School at 105th Northern Boulevard, Queens, New York, to their homes. I did that for about three years, transporting kids from nursery school to the twelfth grade. The children's parents paid me either once a month or every two weeks. I built a kiva upstairs in the school where they prayed every day at noon. I also built a classroom because they were going to rebuild the bathroom and kitchen on the same floor. I would bring them to school around 8:00 a.m., build at the school for $150 a week, and take the children home around 3:00 p.m. There was a fire at the school about two years ago, but I am not sure what happened to the kiva. The principal was Sister Shirley, and the imam, Bakadin, had died. He really liked me, as I must have reminded him of a guy he used to run with. There is a church next door, and after the fire, the church let the school use its facilities.

I came into maturity and developed the spiritual high of recognizing the essence of being a true Native American, and this affected my present physical look. It was like all the spiritual forces surrounding me connected to my families, who were the Native American spirits. When I was a little boy, I looked nothing like an indigene of this land. But one day I looked in the mirror, and I saw an indigenous man. I looked and stared and then realized it was me. I realized what a tall, strong, and handsome indigenous man I had become. I no longer looked like the little boy I used to be. There was a power behind this type of personal physical transformation into my true identity of who I am today. I still can't believe when I look at myself that I turned into the indigenous person I see now. I am no longer the little boy I used to see in the mirror. My cousin Bobby tells me I don't seem like the Junior he used to know. He says I am a different person, and it is like I am a Native American. My sister Elaine, who is a teacher, told my mother I did not seem like their brother. She asked my mom if I really came from her, and she told Elaine yes. But I do not seem like their brother because I look so different from when I was younger and around them.

I know it was the Creator who took me to this second stage of my life, who changed my facial features and my way of thinking into the lifestyle of the Native Americans. My mother had eight children, and I am the only one the Creator chose to trace back into my bloodline through my father. This is why they cannot understand why I act and look different from them as they try to figure out what happened. These inward and outward changes to my person happened before I met Ida, Chief Mayo, the Shinnecock, and the Unkechaug. The Creator himself influenced me and opened my eyes to who I was. Later, he placed me with the tribes from which my ancestors came: Montauk, Shinnecock, and Unkechaug. My ancestors were Mariah Pharoah-Banks and Edward Banks of the Montauk, and Nancy Hudson of the Shinnecock, who was a graduate of Oberlin College. It was meant for me to search for and learn my family's genealogical information. Sarah Ellen Hudson, my paternal second-generation great-grandmother, was born Cherokee in Indian Territory (Georgia) and was listed in the Cherokee Rolls book. My cousin Vivian also found Sarah Ellen Hudson on the 1883 Hester Roll (#2287) of the Cherokee North Carolina Rolls book.

The Hudson and Banks lines are all on my father's side. My cousin Donnell Shinholster in Detroit said our grandmother, Alberta Ashley-Banks, who was a granddaughter of Sarah Ellen Hudson. He told me our relative Edward Banks owned almost all the Montauk lands and that the Georgia Banks were related to the Montauk and Shinnecock. Edward Banks's family migrated from Virginia to New York, and some went to Georgia, Florida, Michigan, and Illinois. Mariah Pharoah-Banks, Edward Banks's wife, was full-blood Montauk Indian from Montauk, New York. She went to Washington, DC, to fight for the return of the Montauk lands to the original Native peoples. The Banks and the Hudson families lived on the Shinnecock Reservation, South Hampton, New York. My people could read and write back in the day, as they were very intelligent.

MONTAUK INDIANS, LONG ISLAND, NEW YORK. LEFT TO RIGHT STANDING: CHARLES FOWLER, JOHN H. FOWLER, POCOHONTAS PHAROAH, AND SAMUEL FOWLER. SITTING: MARGUERITE FOWLER, GEORGE FOWLER AND MARIAH GENEVA PHAROAH-BANKS. SHARED ON ANCESTRY.COM PUBLIC FAMILY TREE BY JUANITA MEDBURY WALKABOUT JULY 2014

My cousin Vivian discovered information about Sarah Ellen Hudson and Henry B. (Prince) Hudson, her husband. John Banks, my paternal grandfather, owned a lot of land in Twiggs County, Georgia, and it could not be sold. Somebody has to show me some paperwork to determine if my father's portion of the land was sold, and if so, to whom. I also know when it comes to money and land, your own family can get greedy and tell you things without showing you any paperwork. My next move is to go to the Bureau of Land Management and find out if my father sold any land and to get some written proof if he did. A lot of times, when you live in the North, people in the South don't think you are interested in anything. I just want to find out if I have a share in this land matter. White and black people worked on my grandfather's (John Banks Jr.) land and at his lumber yard. He had a lot of money, and both blacks and whites would borrow money from him. There are still a lot of Banks living in Dry Branch, Twiggs County, Georgia and they were once in construction. I knew nothing about all this when I was young, but as an adult, I learned more genealogical information from many folks in the family.

[Read more family tree information in the genealogy chapter of this book.]

Meeting Native Americans
Who Look Like Me

———— ℅ ————

I WORKED PART time for Budget Rent a Car in 2003. Three days a week, I drove cars throughout the northeastern region. When I started working at Budget, I found out about my culture in Menlo Park in Long Island, New York. I had carried a group of Pakistanis there for a cultural affair, and I kept wondering about my culture. All of a sudden, I saw this big Indian chief painted on a sheet, and I saw Chief Osceola, Chief Mayo, and Ida. Chief Mayo was born in Riverhead, Long Island, New York, and was a Cherokee. His people were from Virginia. He introduced himself, and I also noticed all these dark-skinned Indians with pretty long hair. They told me I was in Indian Territory, and they were Unkechaug, Shinnecock, and Montauk. I knew the Creator meant for me to see and meet my Native peoples, and I realized Granny Nash was right: we are Indians. These dark-skinned Indians on Long Island had kept the cultural heritage and practices. Granny told me I was Native American from both sides of the family. When I met Chief Mayo and others, I went to his house, and he gave me a rock used by the Indians to make their faces look reddish during the Native American dances.

After I got involved with my people on Long Island, my wife started writing me insulting notes saying, "Heh! You old Indian, go back to the reservation." I should have written to her, "Oh! You Jamaican, go back to Jamaica." Her actions derived from sheer jealousy, and she did not like me because of who I really was and changed to before her eyes. Chief

Mayo warned me that all people, both white and black, would not like me as an Indian. Many light-skinned black women would tell me that they were lighter than me and that I could not be Indian because I am dark skinned. In other words, they could be more Indian than me, whereas the color of one's skin does not make a person a Native, but really it is the spirit and one's genealogy.

Chief Mayo told me he was a Cherokee, as was his wife, Miss Ruth. She told me God sent me there. She knew so because she was a minister and preached in Amityville, Long Island, at a home of some Indians off the reservation. I was feeling so bad that everyone knew their cultures, but I did not know mine. Yet the spirit led me to my people that very day. Little did I know that the Creator would take me to my people, and I have been with them ever since. In later years, a few people started making trouble for me, and I am sure they are not Indians and are just jealous of me. I went with my skills as a painter and carver when Chief Mayo first met me. Chief Mayo and I used to make jewelry, headbands, and chokers together, and we were good at it. I also did paintings and carvings, but he did not.

Next, I met Ida Brewster, a Shinnecock Indian, and she could also make jewelry and different Native American items, such as dresses, vests, skirts, ribbon shirts, and blankets. When I first met Ida, she made me a beautiful red, blue, and white plaid shirt with thunder-birds on each side of my arms and chest. I was very proud that a Native American made this beautiful shirt for me, and I still have it today. After I met and got to know Ida's family, we would go to Sunken Meadow Park in Long Island every year with other Shinnecock, and I was very happy to be around my indigenous peoples. I would take some of my paintings and carvings and sell them to the other Natives who attended this family reunion. These were oil paintings, carved canes, and peace pipes that depicted Native American peoples. I generally like to do my carvings out of white birch and sycamore because the wood is soft and flexible.

CHIEF MAYO IN WHEELCHAIR, ROBERT BANKS CORNELIUS JR.
(CENTER BLUE RIBBON SHIRT), IDA BREWSTER, SHINNECOCK
INDIAN, LONG ISLAND NEW YORK - JUNE 2001

In Chief Mayo's backyard, the spirits led me to carve the faces of ordinary Natives out of a tree trunk. The top of the carving is covered by brown and white deerskin. I have carved fifteen to twenty individual Native American heads and some canes, and people bought them all. Chief Mayo and I would sit in his backyard and carve heads and canes, and people would buy them as fast as I could make them. I would sell a head for $100 and a cane for $60 to $100. I would never sell anything for over $100, even though I knew my carvings were worth $1,000. I tried to be just and not kill them with the price. People always bought my artifacts, and Chief Mayo would shake his head in wonder. My father never wanted me to be an artist. He wanted me to be a baseball player or to study medicine. A baseball player brought home more than the president, who only made $100,000. He would force me to watch baseball games, and to this day, I dislike baseball.

Powwow! I went to a powwow with Chief Mayo, and he wore a long war bonnet that reached all the way down to his ankles. The bonnet's colors were brown and white, and it acknowledged his presence as a ceremony chief, not a reservation chief. I used to walk around with him like I was his bodyguard, and he always felt safe and proud of me walking with him around the Shinnecock Indian Reservation. He was the first man I ever met whereby we had the same identical spirit, and his wife, Miss Ruth, confirmed it. She knew this was true because she is a minister and close to the Creator. We ate, dressed, slept, and woke as Native Americans. Miss Ruth told me the spirit sent me to them. I know we were meant to be chiefs because we held on to our culture and were put on the earth to do so. Chief Mayo passed the war bonnet down to me because I was the only one who would hold on to the culture and remind my family where we came from and who we are. We are not reservation chiefs because we don't live on reservations, but we are ceremony chiefs living off reservations. Once you become a chief, the old ancestors and high spirits give you knowledge of what to do and when to do it. This is why you see me wearing the different silver jewelry that the Creator and the spirits of the ancestors guided my hands to create. It was the same with Chief Mayo, and that is why I know we had the same spirit as we sat at his table making jewelry out of silver and turquoise, whistles out of eagle and buffalo bones, and knives out of deer horns. We also crafted bows and arrows and arrowheads, carved totem poles, and made shirts out of deerskin.

I carved an Indian chief out of a big tree trunk about twenty feet tall on the Poospatuck Reservation in Mastic, Long Island, New York. I go out once a year to maintain it. I also did two oil paintings of Ron's grandmothers on each side of the families, and they are hanging in his house and smoke shop. In the future, Ron will build a new smoke shop, and I will paint murals on the wall. He wants me to do a dream catcher of him and his family. In the future, I would like to do sculptures at the entrance of Poospatuck Reservation. To get there, take the Long Island Expressway, get off at Exit 68, make a right turn, drive to Sunrise Highway, make a left turn (you will see an ice-cream place), make a right, keep riding until to you get to Neptune Avenue, turn left onto Poospatuck Lane, and you are right on the reservation. You will be surprised at what you see: the original Long Island dark skin Natives. It will educate you up to the highest about black Indians, although we don't call ourselves black Indians. To simplify it on all levels, we break it down like that. The Unkechaugs have nice smoke shops where you can buy Indian jewelry, moccasins, regalia, artifacts, and tobacco products. They have powwows once a year just before the Shinnecock powwow. The Poospatuck Reservation is not like it was in the old days; it is now very modern. You will see very modern houses, and the environment is very well kept up. You can go crabbing and fishing right in the reservation's backyard on boats owned by the Unkechaug. If it had not been for Mr. Ron Bell, who recognized my talent to create the sculptures and gave me the opportunity to put them on the Poospatuck Reservation, I would never have been known today, and I thank him for seeing the talent I have in me that I did not recognize I had in myself. My last word about Mr. Ron Bell is, he is a real Unkechaug Indian.

RON BELL, UNKECHAUG INDIAN AND ROBERT BANKS CORNELIUS JR
(WEARING WAR BONNET) ON THE POOSPATUCK RESERVATION - JANUARY 2018

Discovering My Artistic Talents – Learning to Carve with Bama – Poetry and Sculptures

—— ॐ ——

I USED TO sit in Central Park West with a man named Bama who taught me how to carve. He was from Birmingham, Alabama, and taught his daughter and me. Bama, a Creek Indian, led me back to my artwork and enhanced my carving. He, his daughter (a schoolteacher), and his wife would carve African motifs, and I was doing Native American. Bama carved all the famous black singers and stars on a tree trunk, and it is set up in the lobby of the Apollo Theatre. The amateur artists would touch it for good luck before doing their acts on stage. People will do everything but prayer. You mean to tell me Jesus Christ can't hit a curveball? If Jesus cannot hit one, Buddha could never do it. While he did the tree trunk, I was doing a Native American carving out of white birch with Shinnecock motifs on it, which was donated to Fredrick Douglass Academy (1998–99), 155th Street and Adam Clayton Powell Boulevard (Seventh Avenue), Harlem, New York, where my eldest son, Kwadwo, attended and graduated from. The carving is in a showcase in their little museum, and when I went to get it, the principal told me no way, it would not go anywhere because I donated it. I would take these carvings I did every day in Central Park West and sell them fast on the Shinnecock Reservation in Long Island. I met Bama from passing him in my car, and we started talking about being artists, and he told me the layout of carving. One day he said, "Damn, Indian, you catch on fast. It took me a long time to learn how to shape the head, and you learned it practically in a day." The last time I saw Bama was at his house about the year 2003. I saw his daughter one day coming from work on 125th Street, and she told me her father had died. He had a lot of paintings and carvings and was a hell of a poet. He was known as the village poet and believed heaven and hell is right here.

I started writing poetry about twenty years ago. When I attended brush-up classes (reading, writing, and arithmetic) at Columbia University, the professor asked if anyone wrote poetry, and if so, to submit their original poems. Two out of three of my poems were published in soft-cover books for two years while I attended the university. Again, I really never learned anything from any school, including Columbia. I learned more about art from Bama, and he told me sculpting would be much easier than carving. If you can sculpt, you can do anything. You use more muscle when carving with a chisel and hammer, and it also takes more strength. With sculpting, you use your hands more, and you can change the shape of the piece because a hammer and chisel are not used. I write reality poetry about things that actually happen, and it sounds like I am writing a letter to somebody. My poetry deals with everyday life, and there is no rhyme, but it has meaning to it. People have already had experiences with what I write in my poetry. For example, consider the following poem:

WHO?

Who started this mess about
White is right
Yellow is mellow
Brown stick around
And black get back

Have you all took a second thought
And said to yourself
Who started this mess?

And that indigenous people
Of this country
Was the red man
Who started this mess?

I myself is an indigenous Native
Of this country
Do I look red?
Who started all this color mess?

We the indigenous peoples
Of this land
We are still here
And we were never red

I wonder who started this color mess
I wonder who? Who? Who?

Who?

People understand what my poetry means because it's real. Anybody who hears my poetry relates to it and can see it actually happened. I never liked basketball but began to when Dennis Rodman started coming onto the court with different-colored hair. This caught my interest, and I watched him playing the sport. This is the same about people who don't like poetry. When they hear mine, it hits them, they can relate to it, and they usually like it.

My poetry was compiled and published in a softcover book, along with my classmates' poetry, by a professor who taught English at Columbia University. The following poem I consider one of my favorites:

I Had a Dream

I was in the most beautiful place ever seen.
I was walking down this beautiful street.
I saw all the beautiful buildings that were twice as tall as the World Trade Center or the Empire State Building. And when I looked up everything was made out of gold and the street. This seemed for me that this had already been told plus it seemed old.
First, I thought I was on earth, then I realized I was somewhere else. The water was pretty and blue. The trees were tall and that wasn't all. The air was fresh.
My skin was different. Oh! And by the way my skin even looked like gold. But you know what? Something was strange: I did not see a soul but me. This is a true dream. I didn't feel lonely because there was nobody there but me.
But wait a minute; didn't my grandmother tell me one day I would be walking on streets of gold. And that was old because when I leave the earth I already know where I am going because I have been chosen and been shown.
What a beautiful city I have seen that was made out of gold. And if we all do the right thing that is where we will go. So take this tip from me because I have been shown.

I love to travel, and in the future, I plan to go to Europe to see the artworks of Vincent van Gogh, Michelangelo, and Leonardo da Vinci. In January 2010, I started sculpture classes at Fifty-Seventh Street Student Arts League, Manhattan, New York. I was attending Columbia University, and a professor suggested I join this particular art school. My first sculpture art teacher was Anthony Antonios, and the first project I completed under him was Reverend Butts of the Abyssinian Baptist Church, which sits on 138th Street between Lenox Avenue and Adam Clayton Powell Boulevard, Harlem, New York. Reverend Butts' sculpture looks just like him. I proudly presented his sculpture to the congregation on the Family Church Day. Congressman Charlie Rangel was on the premises that day, and everyone was surprised that I, a church member, could do such artwork. My second project was of the late Reverend Ike of the Palace at 175th Street and Broadway, Manhattan, New York, and it looks just like him. I did this project under Anthony too. I also did portraits of Reverends Butts and Ike and donated these art pieces. Reverend Butts proudly displays his sculpture in his office at Abyssinian Baptist Church. The sculpture I completed of the late Reverend Ike cannot be viewed at The Palace because apparently black people don't understand the value of art or appreciate it and show respect to the artist. None of them ever had anyone do a sculpture of them, whether they were black, Asian, white, or any other race. I am an artist and was inspired to do these artworks of the ministry by God so that their great-grandchildren can see them, and they will go down in history.

ROBERT BANKS CORNELIUS JR. AND BARNEY HODES, SCULPTING INSTRUCTOR, STUDENTS ART LEAGUE, MANHATTAN, NEW YORK - FEBRUARY 2018

My third project was life-size statues of President Obama and First Lady Michelle Obama and bust sizes of their two children, Natasha (Sasha) and Malia. Barney Hodes and Anthony Antonios divided their instruction regarding this project. They coached me along, even though I had some knowledge about the artwork. My fourth project, a life-size statue of Michael Jackson, was done under the instruction of Anthony Antonios. Barney and Anthony divided the instruction of my fifth project, a life-size statue of Bruce Lee holding nunchuks. One of my teachers said my sculpture of Bruce Lee was not up to par, even when I brought a sculptured piece of Bruce Lee done by one of the greatest Chinese sculptors in the world. It was proof that I did Bruce Lee right. This gave me confidence and faith in myself and in the God within me and allowed me to stop listening to people telling me crap deliberately. My choice now is to do a self-sculpture, which would probably take me three to four weeks to finish. I want to place it in a museum, such as the National Museum of the American Indian at the Smithsonian in Washington, DC, so that my sons and grandchildren can see it.

ELIZABETH ALLISON, CASTING INSTRUCTOR, AND ROBERT BANKS CORNELIUS JR. OPENING HIS CASTED SCULPTURED BUST, STUDENTS ART LEAGUE, MANHATTAN, NEW YORK - JUNE 2016

The casting instruction for all my projects was by Elizabeth Allison and Steve Marder. They both can do sculpture and casting and are very good people and highly intelligent. I like working with them. Anything they saw that was wrong, they made me tear down and do again. If I had to do it twenty times, I tear it down and do it again one hundred times. I appreciate their generosity and that they want me to do things right while educating me to be an expert caster and sculptor. Anything taught at this school, such as painting, drawing, metalwork, carving, and sketching, Elizabeth and Steve can do. They really enhanced and enriched my art skills, and I very much have to give them high honors. I will do a life-size sculpture of myself. The idea came to me one day that I should do this. If I can sculpt other people, I can certainly do myself because I have been living with myself all my life. I will sculpt myself in full Native American regalia. I plan on putting it in some museum where my grandson and great-grandson can see who I was. I first asked other people to sculpt me, but they seemed hesitant and afraid to do it. The spirit spoke to me and said I can do the life-size sculpture of myself. I will proceed with it, and I know it will come out OK.

ROBERT BANKS CORNELIUS JR. AND STEVE MARDER, CASTING INSTRUCTOR, STUDENTS ART LEAGUE, MANHATTAN, NEW YORK - FEBRUARY 2018

I have to say something about Steve, who is assisting me, despite how much I thought I knew about sculpting. I still have not reached the level of Steve's scholarship and genius. He is a sculptor and a good caster. If it were not for Steve and Beth, we would be lost when it comes to casting. Steve left early one day, and when he came back the next day, he noticed I had put the chains for Bruce Lee's nunchuks in the center instead of on each end. I had to chip out everything to remove them and then put them in the right place. I thought he was trying to bust my chops, but now I realize he is trying to make the best out of me. He always told me to make sure whatever I do it is right and that way I would not have to do it over again. He always tells me to take pride in whatever I do. He and Beth influence me in my life and artwork, and they are the best casters I have ever seen. Beth had a baby boy and went on maternity leave, so Steve and I have been working closely together on my Bruce Lee project. When Beth gets

ROBERT BANKS CORNELIUS JR. AND MAYUMI TAKAGL, CASTING INSTRUCTOR, STANDING BY HIS RECENT SCULPTURE - STUDENTS ART LEAGUE, MANHATTAN, NEW YORK - FEBRUARY 2018

back, she will continue to assist me in the right way to go. Mayumi Takagl is the Cast Instructor in the evening class at the Students Art League, and she is very patient and knowledgeable. When I sometime can not understand her accent she will actually demonstrate the next step in the casting process of my sculpture(s). Casting is another form of art within itself and it is done after an artist finishes creating his/her sculpture.

The God within me guides my hands and does the sculptures for me, because all of sudden, it looks like everything turns to magic. I cannot believe I did all the art projects I've created, and it is because God the spirit guides my hands and does the artworks for me. I am a born artist just like Michael Jackson was a born singer, Michael Jordan was a born basketball player, Tiger Woods was a born golfer, Jackie Robinson was a born baseball player, Joe Louis and Muhammad Ali were born boxers, Louis Armstrong and Buddy B. were born trumpet players, Mahalia Jackson and Ella Fitzgerald were born gospel and jazz singers, Michelangelo was a born sculptor, da Vinci and Van Gogh were born painters, Einstein was a born mathematician, Martin Luther King Jr. was a born orator, Shakespeare was a born poet and playwright, Bruce Lee was a born martial artist, and Geronimo, Sitting Bull, and Crazy Horse were born Native American warriors. So you see, I was put on this earth with a mission to do what I do and do it well. A friend of mine named Terri told me I have eyes like an eagle, and so I named myself Eagle Eye. The following week, the spirit told me the rest of my name is Bear Claw Black and Brown Buffalo. The next week, the spirit told me Eagle Eye Bear Claw Black, Brown, Red, Yellow, and White Buffalo.

Sometimes the people in the art school, such as students or colleagues, have knowledge of something, but if you ask them about it, they refuse to give you any information about anything. I know one thing: I am about to do a six-foot statute of myself, and I will not seek any information from anybody as I have lived with myself all my life. I hope to put it in the National Museum of the American Indian at the Smithsonian Museum in Washington, D.C., and I will see how they like that. I plan on doing the project of myself in the future. I have the Bruce Lee sculpture in the cast. I have taken Michael Jackson out of the cast, and it will take three to four weeks to dry. A cast is when you put three or four inches of plaster on your sculpture and then chip it back out to your sculpture. You use clay to make your sculptured piece, as sculpting is a process. I am sure in the future everyone will see my sculptures all over the world. They will also see my self-sculpture after I am long gone back to heaven where I come from.

The sculpting techniques I use to create a face on my sculptures are the following steps:

1. The end of the eye close to your nose comes down even to the bottom of your nose.
2. The center of the eye comes down to the end of your mouth (lips).
3. The other end of your eye comes down to the bottom of your cheekbone.
4. The ear is at the top of your eyelids to the bottom of your nose on both sides of your head.

ROBERT BANKS CORNELIUS JR. (LEFT) AND THE LATE OLLIE ALEXANDER MAYNES, AN UNKECHAUG INDIAN (RIGHT), STANDING AT THE BACK OF ROBERT'S SCULPTURE, INDIAN CHIEF WITH A PEACE PIPE, POOSPATUCK NATIVE AMERICAN RESERVATION - MAY 2017.

I really take pride in my work as a born artist. I have seven siblings, and as far as I know, I am the only one who is an artist and a poet. I remember that as a child, I would draw all day. So, I will be doing my artwork for the rest of my life. When I go to the Gathering of Nations powwow in Albuquerque, New Mexico, I plan to do an oil painting of the entire powwow. I go there every year, but this is the first time I will do this type of project. I can do a sketch of a thousand people in one to two hours. After I do the sketch, I will start the oil painting, and I will finish on the third day. As a kid, I never knew what my gift was because if you were not a doctor, teacher, or lawyer, then you were a nobody in Atlanta. In Atlanta, they never acknowledge artists, and no matter how good you are, you are looked at as being nothing. I never knew my artistic gift until I came to the North. Everyone was calling me Preacher, but I knew I did not want to be one. To me, being a preacher was not of any value, and I did not want to be that.

My Philosophies of Life and Religious Affiliations

———— ⚭ ————

I WAS ALWAYS into Islam even before I came to New York. Islam deals with science, math, chemistry, and the like, and I was attracted to this faith because of its basic focus on the importance of diet and cleanliness. They talk about what is happening today, whereas Christianity keeps you deaf, dumb, and blind and always talks about what happened two thousand years ago. Christianity tells you all you need is Jesus and does not acknowledge injustice and racism. Dr. Martin Luther King Jr. said that if all the Christians would stand up against racism, it would end overnight. Christianity preaches that we are in the world but not a part of the world. What on earth does this mean? This is why the young people of today don't attend the Christian churches and prefer to become Muslims and honor the teachings of Mohammad. It is untrue that Muslims don't believe in and honor Christ. They do, as well as all the prophets of the Christian Bible. Christianity also preaches that the Ten Commandments were destroyed, but this is a lie because God gave them to Moses to keep mankind on the straight and narrow in their lives today. In the teachings of Islam, black people know more than they do under Christianity, which keeps the evil system of injustice going against people of color. As a child, I realized my grandmother, who went to a Christian church several times a week, was not getting anything out of it, as the preacher called Jesus's name over and over and over, and all the congregation would get pumped up with this type of brainwashing.

I've written Hebrew, Arabic, and Chinese every day for the last twenty years (I've never missed a day). I started this when I separated from my wife and rented a room in a house from Miss Nicholson, who was a preacher. I studied and learned these languages with the help of the Creator. I learned Hebrew and Arabic at the same time in two weeks, and the Creator gave me the knowledge to do this. When a Muslim asked me where I learned Arabic, I told him from Allah. Allah and God are the same person, but the European Christian wants you to think Allah is different from God. This is not true because Allah is in the Arabic language, and God is the same Creator in the English language. I believe in all religions and go to the mosque, the Hebrew Israelite Temple, and the Abyssinian Baptist Church. Of the three, I learn the most from the mosque. Where I am now is through Islam, not Buddhism, Judaism, or Christianity. I was raised in a church, and my aunt Annie Ruth Ross (my mother's sister) was a real preacher and a godsent person who lived with my grandmother Fannie Nash, who told us we are Indian. I am not confused because Jesus and Mohammad taught us to respect and love all peoples. I attended Reverend Ike's church because he talked of love, friendship, happiness, prosperity, and money, which we all need. I do not go crazy over money and don't do stupid stuff to get money. I don't put money over human life, which the average Joe Blow does.

Having God within me stops me from doing crazy things, such as taking advantage of people. That is one thing I like about Reverend Ike: he talks about the God within and that the kingdom of heaven lies within you. If you study the scriptures, Christ said the same thing, that the kingdom of heaven is within you, but the church does not teach this. One thing people don't know about me is that I am a highly spiritual man, and most of what I got in life came not from man but from the highest spirit, God the Creator, ever since I was a kid. I liked school but never learned anything because I am on a higher plane and force. I liked the smell of the school, the pencils and paper, sitting at the desk, and the teachers, but I never learned anything from kindergarten through high school. Even with the art school I presently attend, I go there because I like to see others doing sculptures and paintings and because I enjoy the art environment, but I am not learning anything from anybody. I went with my art skills and knowledge, but the teachers mess up my work, which I have to redo, so I have not learned anything from them.

I know a deep, dark secret: that there was a time when Native Americans of this country were dark-skinned people. They became light-skinned after the European men lie with our women. After two or three hundred years, the Europeans claimed they were "us." We were black like Africans, but we are *not* Africans. A famous writer said, "If the Indians were light-skinned they would never have been surprised to see the white man," and he was right; the Native Americans were black people. You readers must understand that most people don't know this. The Native Americans were never red, brown, or yellow; they were black. True Native Americans have type O blood, and a white medical doctor told me he knew I was Native American because I have type O blood.

When I tell someone I am a Native American of this country, the first thing most think is that I don't want to be black. Then they ask me who is black in my family, and I tell them every damn body. We are still indigenous to this land, but we are not Africans. When the first European set his foot on this soil called Turtle Island, we were all dark-skinned peoples but were never told so in books. I don't know what most people mean when they separate black and Indian instead of saying Native American and African because both of them are black. I realized that most things people don't know they think don't exist because they don't know it. With what you know, you could write a book, and with what you don't know, you could write a library. There are thirteen reservations that still exist on Long Island: the Poospatuck, Shinnecock, Mathinecock, and Montauk. In Connecticut you have the Pequot and the Mohegan, and in Rhode Island you have the Narragansett. All these Indians are black-looking peoples, and they are the original peoples.

Because the Europeans have mixed with us, we look fair-skinned today. If I could trace our family tree to find that anyone is from Africa, I would be glad to accept it, but from what I have traced, we come from here on Turtle Island.

I love Africa and eat their foods, such as fufu (a green leaf that is chopped and ground up, and when it is boiled, it becomes like a dough), all the time. I would like to have me some fufu with some curried goat or lamb dipped in peanut sauce, as this food makes you very strong. So you see, no one is responsible for what race they are. We are all on this earth to get along with one another and not to have conflict because a person is of a different race from you. Who started it? Man! I remember when my grandmother told us we were Indian, and I said to her, "How can we be? Can't you see I'm black?" and she said, "I can see, but remember you came from me. They don't come too much blacker, but so what? You are still an Indian." But as I watched Europeans playing Native Americans on the black-and-white TV, I thought that is what they look like, not knowing I am the original indigenous of this country. I can remember I would say to Momma, "How come we are dark like the rest of the children we are playing with?" And she would say, "They are dark, but they are not Indian. Some of them did come over here as slaves, but we did not. We are from here." I had no problem with Momma telling me this, especially when she told me her father was dark and had two long braids and would sit on the porch carving. She told my sisters, my brother, and me, but it did not seem to touch them like it touched me spiritually, as this was meant to be—I always knew I was chosen. It ain't the clothes you wear that make you indigenous. It is who you really are and the spirit within you. I always had the indigenous spirit from birth because I was chosen. I did not make myself Indian by wearing Indian clothes. I was born this way and chosen by the high spirit and the ancestors to carry on the indigenous American tradition.

I carve and paint Native Americans, and I've sculpted Geronimo and did a self-painting of myself wearing my ceremonial bonnet. I attend the Gathering of Nations Powwow every year in Albuquerque, New Mexico.

The funny thing about it is that when the Southwest Native Americans see me, they always call me Chief, even without my regalia on. I guess they pick up my spirit, and when I ask why they call me Chief, they say I look like a chief. I was just satisfied with being a Native and never wanted to be a chief. Whether Chief Mayo had a plan for me or not, the Great Spirit chose me from birth, but it happened through Chief Mayo. Those who are preachers picked up on my spirituality and wisdom and knew I was going to be somebody of significance in my life. I knew I was not going to be a preacher. My aunt told me I was going to do something special—she saw this as a shadow and could not explain it completely. Now that I am a mature man, she saw me becoming who I really am. Nobody could stop me, as the Creator chose me. He used Chief Mayo as a vessel so that he could put in writing that he passed his Indian headdress to me, and before his death, he told me to wear it proudly. This was not something I asked for; it was passed down to me. There are people who are jealous of me and wonder where I come from. It ain't their business where I come from. I come from the Creator. I don't care how jealous they are; they did not select me for this crown. The Creator did. Whenever the Creator gives you something, man often wonders why and who selected me to have the Indian headdress. They did not give it to me, and they cannot take it away from me.

So you see, I know where my help comes from: it comes from heaven above. I am a special person, and I was selected by the Creator. Man did not give this title that I have. The Creator did. If I were to wait for man to give this title, I would not be an indigene of this country. If it were left up to man, I would be an African with my dark skin. Who are they to tell me who I am? I listen to the Creator. So you see, this is how I know who and what I am: because the Creator showed me. I pray to the Creator day in and day out that he might teach me to speak, like he taught me to write Hebrew, Chinese, and Arabic as well as the languages of the Cherokee, Seminole, Creek, Navajo, Pueblo, Apache, Unkechaug, Montauk, and Shinnecock. If I keep praying to the Creator, I have faith that I will speak all the languages my ancestors once did. I found out things that man keeps from you. You have to go to the Creator for knowledge, and sometimes he sends a person to give the knowledge to you. It can be any race of people, such as Japanese, Chinese, or Native American, who gives you different knowledge. The more I do sculpting, the more things come to me as though through a spiritual connection. Just as Farrakhan has said, sometimes you did not do something, because it was actually Allah who did it and not you.

I felt like a fish out of the water at the age of sixteen when I came to New York City. Around the age of sixteen, I attended Malcolm King Community College in the Hotel Theresa on Seventh Avenue between 125th and 124th Streets. I studied the basic math, science, reading, and social studies courses. I realized this still was not me. So then I got a job in downtown New York City waiting tables. My next was delivering packages. Being a country boy, when I first came from the South, I wore moccasins. A retired Jewish man in his eighties told me to get thick-soled shoes because I was not in the South anymore. In two weeks, I had large calluses on my feet from walking eight hours a day delivering packages in New York City. I wish had taken his advice then because for the rest of my life, I've had bad calluses. Being a country boy, I was hardheaded. I am really glad I came to New York. It is a shame that I had to come to New York to find out that art is just as valuable as being a doctor, lawyer, or schoolteacher. In the part of Georgia I came from, you were not recognized if you were a carpenter or bricklayer. In other words, if you went to Carver Vocational High School, which was a trade school I attended, you would be considered a dummy for learning a trade. There were no art schools in Atlanta, but by the gift of God, having the skills of a carpenter and bricklayer brought out my art skills, which became of value in later years when I attended the Art Students League of New York. Also, my friends who were skilled like me wound up drunks because they were viewed as nobodies or nothings, and they never traveled out of Georgia like I did. When I came to New York, I worked with Europeans and realized they put value on art and other skills. When I attended the carpenters' school downtown on Hudson Street, and I saw again how Europeans put value on carpentry, I knew then that I was just as important as a doctor, lawyer, or teacher.

I used to always want to know why people wanted to go to white schools, and now I do know: because they teach, uplift, and enhance your skills. At the all-black schools I attended in Georgia, the black teachers did not promote or encourage you to be an artist. I know some of you might say this not true, but where I came from in Georgia, this was my experience. My sixth-grade teacher, Miss Hill, told me I would never be anybody and that we would all be down in a hole digging and looking up at the white man saying, "Yes, sir." I always knew I was a good artist and would not be digging holes and looking up at any white man saying, "Yes, sir." I was never discouraged by what Miss Hill told me because I knew that one day I would be somebody through my art skills. The spirit used to tell me that I have God every time Miss Hill would tell me the same crap, and I always felt good and knew I was going somewhere when the spirit insisted that I don't listen to her, as I have God. My grandmother used to always tell us to pray to God to keep us strong mentally and physically and to always believe that you got God and you will succeed in life. So you see, I am writing my autobiography now, and I am a carpenter, a poet, an astrologer, a master mason (I can build a house), and an artist. So now what, Miss Hill? I guarantee she could not do any of this and is now dead. I wonder if Miss Hill realized I would know all this when she said I wouldn't be anybody.

Astrology is dealing with the human body. The first sign is Aries the lamb, which deals with the head and brain. The second sign is Taurus the bull—the neck. The third sign is Gemini the twins—two arms. The fourth sign is Leo the lion—the heart. The fifth sign is Cancer—two breasts. The sixth sign is Virgo—the stomach. The seventh sign is Libra (justice)—two kidneys. The eighth sign is Scorpio—private parts. The ninth sign is Sagittarius (which I am, half horse and half man; with the bow and arrow, we shoot straight to the stars)—two hips. The tenth sign is Capricorn the goat—the knees. The eleventh sign is Aquarius—two ankles. The twelfth sign is Pisces—two feet. What they don't tell us is the ten fingers on your hands are the Ten Commandments, and before you die, you see all the commandments you broke reflected in your fingernails. That is some heavy stuff.

Astronomy is when I look up into the sky and see the stars. I see more than the Big and Little Dippers, as my knowledge goes much farther than that. I can look at the stars whenever I want to learn a language, and I see every language on the face of the earth up in the stars. So you see, I have been well blessed, and my teachings come from the heavens above. I had a dream that I was in heaven, and I was one of those chosen to come down and help build the pyramids in Egypt. The blueprint was in each one of our eyes as human beings. A straight line was placed on the right side of the eye, and we would go back up and raise our hand again, and a straight line would be placed on the left side of our eyes. We would raise our right hand to the Creator, and he would send us to earth to build the pyramids. The formation of the pyramid was between our eyes (the all-seeing eye on the dollar bill). I got scared, and the Creator told me to go back to earth, where I have remained since. I know I come from heaven, and this where I am going back to. We moved the stones of the pyramids that weighed tons without touching them by using mental telepathy (our minds).

I was the same person and looked just like I look now when I was doing the pyramid building. But when I was sent back to earth, I could no longer return to heaven because I was still scared and not ready to go back, so I had to remain on earth. So you see, you all talk about coming from heaven, and I actually have been there. I know some of you who are reading this book might ask, "What is this guy talking about? He comes from heaven and built the pyramids?" Whether you believe it or not, it is true, and I know where I come from and will go back to. I know this seems like a lot, and you are probably wondering, "Does this guy actually believe that?" It ain't that I actually believe it but that I know where I come from. Earth is not my home; heaven is.

I came down here to complete a mission: to let you know that there are other planets besides earth and that there are other worlds within the universe. There are other, bigger and bigger, galaxies. I come from one of them out there. This is one reason why I came down here to write this autobiography: to let you know people come from other places. The Creator sent me through my mother, who was the vessel, but I am so different from my other siblings. All she could tell everybody is what an intelligent son she had, even though she did not know I came from heaven. This is why the people called me Preacher because they saw the godly person I am, as well as the good in me, not knowing where I came from but seeing something different in me. The good they saw in me was that I am a Native American bringing back what the indigenous peoples had lost. This is my mission. When the Europeans gave them Christianity, they lost their identity. This is why they thought I was going to be a preacher and not a ceremonial chief, which is a high spiritual person. You don't have to be a preacher to be a righteous person. You have to be spiritual and a good person to treat humanity right. Treat your brothers and fellow men as you would want to be treated, no matter their color. This biggest problem on earth is people dealing with color instead of right and wrong, which has nothing to do with color. People can be your own color and still kill you. A person can kill you even if he or she is your race.

I visit my ancestors on different planets. I don't travel back and forth in my whole body and soul like I did in the past. Now I go only in my spirit form—for example, when I go to sleep, I travel to visit my ancestors. These ancestors don't like what you all are doing on earth, killing one another. One day you've got to leave this earth, face the Creator, and pay for what you have done. You all are killing one another as though you will be here forever, but you are going to have to pay for your wrongdoings. Believe me, buddy, there is another world outside of this one. In fact, there are billions of them out there. Which one are you going to end up in? If you have not treated your brothers and sisters right, then you are certainly not going to end up in a very nice world. I don't mean to preach to you all because I am not a preacher. I am just telling you the facts.

EAGLE EYE AUTHENTIC OFF RESERVATION CHIEF LETTER FROM CHIEF MAYO

I am an off-reservation chief, and I have twelve senses, which are my kundalini, or my lower backbone. Each notch of the spine is one of your senses up to your head, and my queen chakra is in the center of my head. I can see into the invisible world that the average person cannot see into. I was born with this gift. This is why I know all these things. I am not just talking off my head but stating a fact. I can see what is going on all over the world, and I don't have to be there. Why are you reading this book? Don't try to figure me out. Figure yourself out and whether you are going to be a good person or a bad person and mistreat people. Remember, you have two spirits in you, a good one and a bad one, and it is up to you which one you want to use. The good one is the Creator himself, and the other is Satan himself. They both dwell in the mind.

Because good things are not done by man alone, I would first make an offering and send my voice to the spirit world that it may help me to be truthful. I fill the sacred pipe (like a peace pipe) with the bark of white birch that I carve with. Before we smoke it, you must see how the peace pipe is made and understand its meaning. There are four eagles on the pipe, which represent the four corners of the universe. First, the black eagle to the west represents wisdom, knowledge, and understanding. Next, the red eagle to the east represents goodwill to all men, harvest, corn, and fish. The brown eagle to the south represents wisdom, power, and growth. Last, the white eagle to the north represents rain, snow, wind, and cleanliness. I know you're wondering where I got the eagles' different colors, but remember that I can see into the spiritual world and you cannot. The symbol of the eagle defines how man's mind should be high. Do you realize that man's thoughts travel twenty-four billion miles per second and that you have fourteen billion brain cells? Most people label Native Americans based on color. The biggest secret about Native Americans is that we are close to the Creator, and this is where we get our knowledge, wisdom, and understanding. We are taught by the Creator to treat all creatures, as well as mankind, the same.

We Native Americans don't look at skin color the way other races do. An Indian is like this: if you don't like me, then I don't like you, no matter what color you are. We like people who like us. I have people ask me all the time how I know I am an Indian. I tell them I know I'm Indian because the Creator told me I am *not* man. It is also in my nature. I eat like an indigenous, I dress like an indigenous, and I think like an indigenous. I got the spirit of an indigenous person. I worship my peace pipe, and I pray to the Creator each and every morning, never missing a day. Also, I am good with my hands, and I am good with colors. Being a Native American ain't just putting on Native American clothes. You must have the spirit of a Native American, and then you know you are one. We, the true Indians, call them one-day Indians when they come to a powwow dressed like a Native and the next day they put on Western-style clothes. That is not the Native way. If you are a Native, then you are going to be just like me: you are going to look, act, and dress Native. I don't give a damn who doesn't like it because I am a Native!

I have had some people come up to me and give me a problem. They don't know anything about my ancestors or me. It is their first time ever seeing me, and yet they try to create problems for me. But they don't know I am very dangerous. When they come up to me with their nonsense, they don't know they are playing with fire. This ain't only the outside people. There are those who claim to be Indians but have no proof. These are who I call the want-to-be Indians, who always want to cause problems for me. Lying on me, pretending I am saying this or that, and wanting me to look bad in other people's eyes. I never have problems with real indigenous peoples, for they realize who I am. I don't have to explain anything to these people who try to make problems for me because they've never seen a damn dark Indian. It never was the color of one's skin that makes a person. It is their spiritual connection to the Creator. When the Creator blesses you, there is a lot of jealousy. Every blessing has a devil behind it, and I ain't talking about a devil in the ground, as there is no such thing. I am talking about the devil who eats, sleeps, drinks, put on clothes, and goes to work, church, and school just like everybody else. He or she is five or six feet tall, fat or skinny, with curly, straight, or nappy hair, and comes in all different colors. So all of you should smile behind this one because everything is true and there is nothing spooky about an indigenous person because we deal with reality, the real stuff. I might be polite to those who are against me, but what they don't know is I am a black belt in karate, will use a gun if I have to, and will fight them any kind of way they want. If they grab a weapon, I will too. I would grab my bow and arrow and use that on them too.

I admire the Reverend Joyce Myers and used to watch her daily as one of my favorite ministers. I really love the fact that she is a woman minister. What I like best about her is when she would say, "Don't be so quick to want to get blessed because once you get blessed, there are a lot of devils come behind it with a lot of lies." I watched her on TV before this happened to me, as she is very down-to-earth and a good minister. She speaks in the past tense and the present tense and is not like the average preacher today who is afraid to talk about the realities of life. She is a very brave woman. Nevertheless, I cannot let these lies stop me, as this is something God blessed me to do; he chose me. The spirit that chose me is not a weak being, and neither am I. If they keep up with these lies, they are going to find out what spirit is behind me. I was always willing to do just things for all Native peoples, no matter the tribe they were from. I had made an oath to do just Native stuff, which is why I currently have over 450 paintings of all Native peoples, including a few sculptures made from tree trunks and buffalo hides. My youngest son, Ali, told me to do other peoples, as I have so much trouble with the want-to-be Indians. If they had come to me, I would have shown them how to do what I do. But because these Negroes who are not Indians caused me trouble, I refuse to show them anything. This is when I chose to do a sculpture of President Obama. I broke my oath, but I really expanded within myself by doing artworks of other peoples and cultures.

So you see, you always have a bunch of devils around trying to stop progress. The thing about it is they get all involved with these tribes, going from place to place and putting out rumors that I said I was a chief of all different reservations, which was the biggest lie ever told. I am still going to do things for the Native peoples and for other peoples—those who appreciate what I am doing for them, and I don't worry about them going around lying. I noticed that you can say you are a Jew or you can say you are white and be black as coal, and there is not a problem. You can be jet black and say you are Chinese or Japanese, and there is no problem. But when your skin is dark and the minute you are a Native American, there is always a problem. What is wrong with this picture? I am a Native of this land. My skin is dark, and I don't give a damn about anyone's opinion because I know who I am, a Native American.

Remember, the Creator chose me and not man. If it was left up to you all to choose me, this is the problem I would be having. Don't worry about where I come from; I did not just come here and you all started seeing me. I have been here. This sort of reminds me of when I was in elementary school. I was a very smart student and did not mess with anybody; I just did my artworks. But all of a sudden, the kids decided to start picking on me. Then I started fighting and beating up everyone, and I became the bad kid in the projects. So you see, people should mind their business and stay out of other people's business. This is what starts major problems. There is an old saying in the Bible that you are all familiar with: "Don't worry about getting the splinter out of someone's else's eye; worry about removing the log out of your own eye." I got 450 paintings now in my house and would drop every last one the same way I dropped my books in elementary school; for every painting I got, I would kick 450 asses. I know I am going to win because I am a Native American possessing the Great Spirit within.

All the Christian preachers talked nothing about dietary habits or about who you were. All they mentioned was Jesus one thousand times, and yet you learned nothing about Jesus or yourself, only that you were going either to heaven or hell, and I could never relate to that. Later, I came to New York and heard about Malcolm X and Marcus Garvey, so I had three people to admire: Elijah Muhammad, Malcolm X, and Marcus Garvey. Then I met Reverend Ike, whom I could really relate to and who inspired me, along with the others. I learned later that Elijah Muhammad is related to me. He came from Sandersville, Georgia, the same place my maternal grandmother, Fannie (née Burt) Nash, was from. I was told this at a family reunion in Macon, Georgia, in 1986–1987 with the Banks and Cornelius families. My other heroes are Geronimo, Crazy Horse, Sitting Bull, and Osceola. I was so amazed by these guys. I would be so hurt as a kid watching the movies that showed the Europeans killing them. This is why I always felt like I was a Native since I was a kid, and after my paternal grandmother told me who I was, it triggered everything.

As an adult, I spent time researching my ancestors and who I am. I had no time to study about other Indians as I am one myself. I could never figure out as a child how the big, fat, whiskered white Santa Claus would come down the chimney. How could he deliver toys to children all around the world in one night? Just like I could never understand why Christ had to die to save the world, but I was not living during that time. Why did he have to die for us, and the white man was doing bad things to us, and yet we were supposed to be the sinners? The whites enslaved us, and Christ died for us as the sinners. I could not understand about the devil in hell with a pitchfork and that we were going to hell while the Europeans were giving us hell on earth; we were catching hell twice. I would say we were not to speak our Native American language, and we still have to suffer at the hands of the Europeans who were supposed to be saved by Christ and who were doing wrong to us. I was four years old and could analyze all this. So you see, as I got older, I found out there is no devil in the ground, but there is a high spirit that causes the sun to shine, the wind to blow, the harvest to feed us, and the four different seasons. Using my common sense, I realized there has to be a higher spirit to feed mankind so that we can survive on earth.

But we've also got a good and an evil spirit that live within us. The good spirit lives in man for us to do the right thing while we are here on earth. Then you got a bad spirit that lives within human beings. They claim the bad spirit is the devil in the ground, but he always walked around with shoes and clothes. You never see somebody come out of the ground to kill man. Everybody you see doing bad things is human and not invisible. Heaven and hell remains within you, and whichever one you wish to live in is up to you. You can go out and kill, and the consequences are up to you. I am glad that God lives within me, and whoever reads this book better take heed where God and the devil live. The Creator always has and always will work in man. Nothing was kicked down from nowhere; you had the high-spirit mind but chose the low-spirit evil mind. All this stuff I am telling you in this book is top secret.

It is up to you whether to use either the good or the bad, but speaking for myself, I'd rather use the good to live with the God in me. From now on when you see people doing bad things, it is the devil they told you was in the ground. When you see people do good, it is the high spirit within them who allows them to do this. So all this stuff about what color God and Jesus are does not matter because God lives within the hearts and minds of us all. Also, the devil lives in your heart, and the color does not matter. It never has been a color thing, black, white, or red. It has always been what spirit you choose, whether good or bad, and that relates to what color it is. It relates to any damn color; you can be evil or you can be good. To give you a good example, the idea that the devil is in the ground holding a pitchfork, that was the devil himself fooling the masses of people. Nobody thought of this because they are still preaching the crap, and it does not resonate with the young people of today. This is why the young people do not sit up in churches.

By the way, by me being a Native American of this country, we never went for that story about the devil. We always knew who the devil was and where the good and bad spirits lie. You never saw anything invisible doing evil, such as using a gun, dropping bombs on people, taking land from people, taking people from their land, and making them slaves who work for nothing. It is always somebody you can see doing these things. When I was a little boy, I noticed my mother never talked crap about the devil. She was not that educated herself, but she had sense enough to know that we should be educated and always told me about my grandfather and our Native American heritage. We still don't know what Indian was from my mother's side. When I was older, I did more family genealogy research and found out that, on my father's side, the Banks were on the Shinnecock, Montauk, and Poospatuck Reservations, as was the Hudson family. It was something like a circular connection, whereby family members went all over from Virginia, New York, Ohio, Michigan, Illinois, and Georgia. People try to tell you that because the Banks are all over we are not related, but that is stupid because we have the same damn name.

I have not run into any Hudsons, but I do know I come from the Hudson family because my second-generation great-grandmother was Sarah Ellen Hudson. I will be going on the Montauk, Shinnecock, and

Poospatuck Reservations to look for genealogical information about the Hudson family. It really surprised me because when I looked in the Cherokee North Carolina books, I found out the Hudsons were from the Eastern and Western Bands. This confused me, so I called a cousin in Detroit. He told me they were from the Montauk and Shinnecock areas on Long Island, New York. Our grandmother told him that is where we came from. I am related to these tribes by both blood and marriage. You see how family information can get screwed up. I had to do genealogical research to get the written information, in addition to the oral information told us by our grandmother Alberta Banks Cornelius (née Ashley). But nevertheless, I am the one chosen by the Creator to bring out the real truth and to present it to the family in this book. At this time I teach the Indian culture to the family. I dress Native, eat Native, and sleep Native, and I am the only one in the family keeping up the culture through my sculpting, painting, and jewelry making.

Everything I got and everything I know comes from the Great Spirit. I have had quite a few people ask me how I know I am an Indian. I told them the Great Spirit told me who I am. By the Great Spirit, I do *not* mean a loud voice booming down from the heavens saying, "This is the Great Spirit"; it doesn't work like that. He speaks to you through your thoughts, and when you have good thoughts that work, you know it was the Great Spirit who gave you the thoughts. As an example, I am an artist and a poet and good with numbers. When I come up with a poem, I know it was the spirit telling me what to say. It is the same with oil painting; he shows me the right colors to use on my paintings. Also, with my sculpture, I can look at the face only, and he shows me the back, sides, and elevation. Remember, a human is four dimensions, but I can just look at the face from a photo, and the Great Spirit shows me all the other dimensions. The Creator gives me my numbers through dreams, and when I play them, they always come up. The numbers are a gift from the Creator.

So you see, you don't have to depend on man for anything. You must pray to the high spirit, and he will answer your prayers. Depend on the high spirit, as man will lead you wrong because of jealousy. Don't forget that. A funny thing about jealousy and being prejudiced is that it makes you look very ugly. It shows up all over your face, and you can't hide it. I've learned that people of color are not that prejudiced against other races, but they seem to have problems with one another. I noticed European peoples and other groups who are not prejudiced toward the dark races of peoples look beautiful. Most professional people like doctors and lawyers (not crooked lawyers) look better. They look more aristocratic and have better personalities when interacting with other ethnicities. We can always come up with excuses that we are black, white, and so on. That is crap because you can only stop yourself with excuses. Nobody can stop you from doing what the Creator has given you to do on this earth.

Any race of people who try to hold another race down has to be down there with them and thus is holding their own race down. For example, if you and I are wrestling and I have to hold you down, then I have to be down there with you. So you see, people have got to cut out all this stupidity. I used to think in life that it was only the Europeans who were against people of color, only to find out there are also people of color against one another. There is more in this world than just black and white. The biggest secret kept back is that the Native people are black people; they came in all shades and were never white. They were jet-black, brown, and reddish, but they were never white.

One time a guy told me I was the first black Indian he had ever seen. I told him if he stuck around, then he would see a lot more. He was a man in his eighties who said he was a Native Cherokee, and he was of reddish complexion. But I wondered how he recognized me as being an Indian if he'd never seen a dark-skinned Indian before? Every time he sees me, he calls me Chief. I also noticed black and white people call me Chief. When I went to Albuquerque, New Mexico, everybody—Native, white, or black—called me Chief. It must be something they see in me, owing to the fact that I was picked by the Creator himself. I just look like the Shinnecock, Montauk, and Unkechaug tribes. I did not look for these people; the Creator led me to them. It ain't that I think I was chosen—I know I was chosen. One strange experience I recently had involved an on-the-job accident. It appears that those handling my case were prejudiced against me and did not give me the medical treatment I should have had. They seemed to resent me because I am a dark-skinned indigenous person and not what they expected—that is, an African.

I know who I am because the Creator told me so, and I am *not* an African but a dark-skinned Native American. All dark peoples of the world are not Africans and are not the same. You Europeans who are white are of different nationalities and speak different languages. You can even see this in the animal world: a pit bull is not a German shepherd, and a German shepherd is not a Doberman, and yet they all are of the dog species. A lion is not a leopard, and a jaguar is not a panther, but they all are of the cat species. I am simplifying this to show you that just as we have all these different animal species, it is the same with people. Don't think because my skin is black like an African that I am an African and not a Native of this land, as the Creator put me here. Most men are lost themselves, and although they can try to put me on the right track, the Creator speaks to me always and tells me who I am.

I assume that most people don't make their prayers like I do, each and every day. I try not to speak for anybody else, as I don't know what you all are doing. If you don't listen to the God in you, then man will mislead you. The Creator leads me in all that I do and say. I don't just do and say any old thing. I don't know where you all get that you have to look a certain way to be a Native American. The Creator himself chose your nationality, and it does not have a damn thing to do with your color or hair. I have had people ask me, "Ain't you got black blood in you?" I tell them, "Don't you see how black I am? I am black." Most people have a noun mixed up with an adjective. This whole system is wrong: the red man, the black man, the white man, and the yellow man. It is a bunch of garbage, and it doesn't make you who you are. The biggest problem people have with themselves, not with me, is that I don't want to be black. I tell them, "Don't you see how black I am? They don't come any blacker than me." If color had anything to do with who I am, I'd rather be black.

When you tell someone you are an indigenous person of this land, most think that you are denying your black African roots. I tell them Africans are not the only black people in the world. I had one guy come up to me from one of the islands, Jamaica or Trinidad. He asked me what made me think I am a Native American, and I told him it is the way I think. He said, "You mean to tell me if I think like a white man, it means I am a white man?" I told him, "First of all, if you think or have the spirit of a white man, then that is what you are. Forget about the color of your skin. The Creator said so as a man thinks, so is he. He did not say so as your color, so is you." I'm not making this up. It's in the Bible you all believe in. Don't worry if you are thinking you are not that. If you ain't got the spirit in you, you are not going to think that way regardless of your color.

I found out that most people who know they are Native American try to hide because they don't want to be black. If they do dress up for a day or two as Native Indians, it is not in their spirits. They don't dress like I do as a Native American every day or even shop for Native clothes that I wear to more than just a powwow. They like being a Native American but are ashamed of what people will say about it. They don't have the inner pride and spirit to be Native American, and everybody you run into is a damn Cherokee, as if it is the only tribe that exists. I am a Cherokee on my father's side and Muscogee Creek, Montauk, Shinnecock, and Unkechaug through the Banks and Hudson families. The last two families mixed with the Cherokees in Virginia and moved to Georgia. I have learned a lot about my families' Native American heritage within the last year. It was confusing because I could not see how they were of all these tribes, but my first cousin Donnell Shinholster, who lives in Detroit, explained it to me. He was born in Macon, Georgia, and lived with his grandmother Alberta. It was his mother who told him about the Banks's connection with the Shinnecock, Montauk, and Unkechaug tribal peoples.

When I started attending powwows thirty years ago, the first one I went to was the Shinnecock in 1980 with Chief Mayo. I was so amazed when I met Native Americans who looked like me. I did not participate in the Grand Entry, but when I went to New Mexico in 1995, I danced in the circle of the Gathering of Nations Powwow for the first time. Another interesting thing is that I never knew what kind of Indian I was and so told everyone I was Shinnecock. It wasn't until I was grown and learned who I was that I confirmed I really was Shinnecock on one side. After some research I found out I was related to both tribes. It was amazing to me to meet the peoples of the other tribes at the New Mexico powwow.

Before I met them, I felt like a fish out of water. Once I met them, I felt like I was at home and joined back up with my peoples again. It is a wonderful feeling to know who you are and when nobody has to tell you who you are. I am going to continue on with my culture and the way I live. I notice that other so-called Indians admire me for keeping the culture going. I also attended the Narragansett, Pequot, and Mohegan powwows at the same time I attended the Shinnecock. I started participating in the Shinnecock powwow Grand Entry about the year 2000. I was not wearing the war bonnet then because Chief Mayo was still alive. After he passed it to me, I started participating in the Grand Entry at the Shinnecock pow-wow. This is when people started telling lies on me regarding the war bonnet. I can prove who I am, but I doubt those who started this chaos (the want-to-be Indians) can prove they are Indians. Many of them are just a whole lot of black people starting mess and trouble for no reason at all. Here I am a good person trying to help, and I'm attacked by a bunch of jealous black people and want-to-be Indians who don't know anything about me. I know who I am and don't have to prove anything to anyone. The Creator chose me. Now what? I am protected by the Creator, and the truth always overpowers lies.

I noticed that anybody can come out with a white face, and nobody starts anything with them. The minute they see a dark face, for some reason they think they can start trouble with them. One thing they don't know is that the Creator chose me and that I am an original Native of this land, but they will find this out too. It is enough that the land was taken away from us. We don't need some little Joe Blow want-to-be Indian going from powwow to powwow starting problems because my skin is dark. They figure they can start trouble with me, but little do they know they are treading on dangerous ground because although I act meek and nice, I'm no one to be trifled with. When it comes to my identity and who I am, I don't need anyone playing around and lying. They better mind their business because a real Native is no one to be playing with, and that is me.

I mind my own business. I don't concern myself with anyone else's business, and they should stay out of mine. The Creator chose me, and they don't know anything about that. Whenever you are chosen by the Creator, nobody can touch you. They can try to lie on you and backstab you and do whatever they want to do, but ain't nothing going to work. Whenever the Creator blesses you, you always have enemies for some reason. If they were close to the Creator when making their prayers, then they would be blessed too and know where their help comes from. But because they are so interested in watching me and being jealous of me, they are not making their prayers to the Creator and are missing those blessings. The difference between them and me is that I believe in the high spirit, am not jealous of anyone, and mind my own business. But I do know one thing: if people try to create problems with me, they are treading on dangerous ground.

I am going to keep on with my life, doing my sculptures and oil paintings and keeping up the traditions, because I love doing what I am doing. If I get permission, my goal is to do a ten-foot sculpture for each of the Montauk, Shinnecock, and Poospatuck Reservations. I want to donate these sculptures to these reservations, and I hope one day they will give me permission to do the artwork. But until then I will continue to do my artwork of both Natives and non-Natives. There is a lot that can be done on the different reservations as far as artwork. I know I was chosen by the Creator to do different things for the reservations. All they have to do is give me the OK, and I will put forth the rich artwork that our ancestors were once doing. I would like to sell my completed 450 pieces of artwork on the reservations for a reasonable price. Why do I have so many? I always fall in love with my artworks and never want to get rid of them. Now that I have accumulated so many, I want to sell some of them.

I had made an oath one time that I would do nothing but Native American art pieces, but then it seemed that everybody became jealous of me and started lying, so I began doing other peoples besides Native Americans. This is the biggest problem they have: saying what and who they are doesn't mean anything in this day and age. I am not interested in their nonsense about who I am or who they are because they did not make me. I don't have to be on the reservation or accepted by them because they did not make me. I am still a native of this land, and all I want to do is good for all peoples of this land. Whether or not they accept me and allow me to do my artwork on the reservations, I will continue to do what the Creator has brought me here to do.

Our problem now is that we have to look at the golden times when we indigenous peoples were together. If it wasn't my mission to be doing this here, they would never have known about me, but I was sent by the Creator to be among them to do the artwork that was once cut off from the peoples. We got some old jack shit in the crowd causing chaos for somebody who was chosen by the Creator, and that was me. All they are doing is stopping me from doing things for the reservations. But I do know one thing: once you are chosen by Creator, no man can stop you. He might try, but eventually he is going to vanish into thin air, and I will do what I was chosen to do. Tomorrow is going to be a different day, and the same want-to-be Indians are not going to be around. I will continue to do my work that I was put here to do.

The funny thing is that I did not make this choice myself. I was chosen by the Creator. It is very rare when you can see a man who can do sculpture, oil and sand painting, and carving, plus carpentry—that is, I can build houses. I am a great layout man, and I can do bricklaying. I am not that good with reading and writing, but I am very good in math. I found out I am not missing anything because even the Native Americans who are very highly educated and wrote to the authorities about their land, they still didn't get what belonged to them, so now what? If you look back in history, the Europeans did not get anything due to how well they could read or write. They took everything from the Native Americans by violence. So you see, no matter how good your education, it makes no difference to how the Europeans treat the indigenous peoples of this country. We are still being cheated and denied our land and civil rights. We are still playing this color game by not showing dark-skinned Native Americans, who were the original peoples of Turtle Island. I know I run into a lot of people who ask me if I am Indian. They ask me what kind, and I tell them one side is Cherokee and the other Shinnecock and Montauk.

Some people tell me they've never seen Indians as dark as me. I saw a program on TV about a Pequot who never knew he was an Indian until he was grown. He found out he was an Indian and had all his papers of proof. When they asked him how he knew, he said he got suspicious because he'd never had any communication between the African Americans and the Africans themselves. But he did the research and discovered he was a Pequot. They always showed him talking on TV at 3:00 a.m. so that the regular public would not see it. The interviewer asked him what made him believe he was a full-blood Indian when he looked like an African American. They said he was supposed to get a lot of money, but he never did and later died. A Montauk Indian who lives in Queens, New York, knew the Pequot man and perhaps has the DVD about him. The interviewer asked the Pequot, "What if black people see you? Do you think it would start them to thinking?" The Pequot said, "I think so."

The Montauk Indian asked me, "Do you think the whites were going to give the Pequot man the money and land?" Of course, he would not be given the money and land by the white authorities who had lied and cheated our people for centuries. But due to the fact that the Pequot man did not look like an Indian in accordance with the stereotype of the way Indians are supposed to look, he was not given the money and land. The Indians on the West Coast look different from those on the East Coast. When one indigenous leaves and goes to the other side with the ancestors, you have five more who got the same information, and you cannot kill them out. The European, the so-called white man, has been trying to hide the true identity of the Native Americans on the East Coast ever since he set foot on Turtle Island. But the funny thing about it is that the young kids born today know what the true Native Americans look like.

One day a little boy about five or six years old shouted, "Daddy, Daddy, look at the Indian." His daddy looked at me for a second and then walked over to me and asked, "Are you an Indian?" I said, "If your son told you that, you had better listen because his mind has not been poisoned yet by this world about what the indigenous peoples of this country really look like. You should stop and ask yourself, 'How did my son recognize he was an Indian when I did not know this myself?'" The kids of today are not looking at the old movies in which white people played Indians, so their minds are not poisoned, and they automatically know what the Indians look like. I noticed that older kids around thirteen or fourteen will say, "Whoa, whoa" and make smart remarks because their minds have been poisoned. I don't pay any attention to them and don't get offended at all because they are ignorant of the facts. The older people are even more stupid. I also know why the Creator says we should turn back into kids because they see more and know the truth. Children are innocent beings and know the truth. For all of us, the older we get the more naive we get.

I know a lot of Native peoples who are ashamed of who they are. I don't give a damn what people think about me because I was chosen by the Creator. The ones who are ashamed of their culture were just told; they don't have the spirit in them, and they were not chosen. When you know you are chosen, you don't care what people say about you. This is the difference between them and me because they were not chosen like I was. I call them ashamed of who they are and one-day Indians. They put on their Native American regalia for powwows only. Once you are called by the Creator like I was, you are joined back to the bloodline of your ancestors whom you were once cut off from. You have to listen to the Creator. When the Creator comes to you, you have to listen. Otherwise, if you don't recognize this, you miss your blessing.

You are not an Indian because you put on Native American clothes and go to powwows and dance. I know that I am Indian because the

Creator groomed me and shaped me. Once the Creator grooms and shapes you, everybody can recognize who you are. And the whole secret is that once he came into my life, I recognized it was him. If I hadn't recognized him, I could have missed my blessing. The thing is, when the Creator comes, most don't pay attention to the voice within, which is the Creator. They are too busy listening to the people without. How I know who I am and what I am, and even why people who don't know me call me Chief, is because of the great Native American spirit people see in me, especially other Native Americans themselves. It is a good thing to listen to the spirit within because that is where you get all your answers. I've learned that people who don't see something with their physical eyes don't think it exists. You don't see gravity, but if you go to the top of the Empire State Building and jump off, you will realize that even though you can't see gravity, it's there. Neither can you see the air that you breathe, but it is there. We need air in order to live.

There are thirteen reservations on Long Island, and some who were born on the island never knew this. I can name a few of them, but not all, because many don't exist anymore. You have the Shinnecock, Unkechaug, Mathinecock, Montauk, Setauket, and others. So you see, when the Great Spirit blesses you, he chooses who pleases him, and most people don't acknowledge me because I am one of the chosen ones. Most times when you are blessed, you gain a whole lot of enemies because there is a devil behind every blessing. Before the Creator chose me, I had no enemies because no man gave me anything. Life is like a triangle. You got one line coming from the Creator giving me the knowledge that I then pass on to other people at the bottom of the line. Then the next man goes back up the line to pray to the Creator after I give him the knowledge. I am not there to babysit him; he has to go to the Creator himself. The Creator will give him knowledge to pass on to others. I am very proud who I am, and I did not have to wait for man to tell me who I am. I got my knowledge straight from the Creator. My knowledge is pure. This is why everything I do, and especially what I never did before, I can basically figure out how to do it if I choose to attack the situation.

On February 12 through August 7, 2011, an exhibit titled "RED/BLACK: Related through History" was held at the Eiteljorg Museum of American Indians and Western Art, Indianapolis, Indiana. The exhibit was groundbreaking as it explored the interrelated histories of Native Americans and African Americans, which is a topic that is seldom spoken about or taught in our classrooms. It was impossible for me to attend the opening-day events, but I and Professor Morehand-Olufade did travel to Indianapolis and saw the exhibit on Friday, July 29, 2011.

LEFT TO RIGHT: JAMES H. NOTTAGE, VICE-PRESIDENT & CHIEF CURATORORIAL OFFICER - EITELJORG MUSEUM, PROFESSOR DARNELL A. MOREHAND-OLUFADE, ROBERT BANKS CORNELIUS JR. – EITELJORG MUSEUM OF AMERICAN INDIANS AND WESTERN ART, INDIANAPOLIS, INDIANA – JULY 2011

We were very surprised when we rode into the museum's parking lot and saw a gigantic banner with my photo (the one on the cover of this book) wrapped around the front of the building. When we entered the lower level of the building to take an elevator up to the main floor, again my photo was displayed on a wall outside of the elevator. Two women walked into the elevator behind us, and immediately they recognized me as the person in the photo because I was wearing my war bonnet. They started jumping up and down excitedly and started shaking my hand and hugging me. We got off the elevator together, and they asked me to autograph the REDBLACK programs they picked up as we entered the foyer. Mr. James Nottage, who was the vice president and chief curatorial officer, greeted the professor and me and escorted us throughout the entire exhibit, which was historically informative with beautiful cultural displays. We were told my photo was chosen the "signature" photo of the exhibit and was displayed on the city buses and flags throughout Indianapolis during the exhibit. I called the Washington, DC, National Museum of the American Indian to find out who chose my photo and was told it was a panel of twelve Native Americans who chose it for the REDBLACK exhibit.

My mother had eight kids, six girls and two boys. I follow my eldest sister. None of them have considered who they are, but they know it. Only two of my sisters went with me to the Poospatuck Reservation, but it meant nothing to them. They don't know the blessing that they had to go with me onto a reservation and see Native Americans who look like them, not the stereotypical Indians. Sometimes even though you can take a person to the well, that doesn't mean they will take a drink. I took them to the Poospatuck Reservation where they saw Native Americans who look like them, and they still did not accept this. I have no hard feelings because they were not chosen by the Creator like me, their brother. Maybe it will come through their great-grandchildren. What a wonderful feeling to know who you are and that you were not labeled by man for this knowledge. I have had people ask me, "How do you know you are a Native American?" I tell them the Great Spirit showed me who I am, and they look at me as if I am crazy and laugh at me. Even people who are ignorant laugh at me, but intelligent, godly people know what I am saying is the truth. So you see, I am going to keep on keeping on and doing what I am doing because we, the Native American people, are still here. We are not going anywhere because the Creator put us here for our food with the wild game and berries in the forests and the fish in the oceans and rivers, and we know exactly what to do.

The Europeans thought they bought the land and the air too, but that same air is still here, and the land and air are like husband and wife. They have not bought either one of them. We were made from the dirt of this land, and the Creator put us here, so you can't get rid of us ever, as no man is above the Creator. If it wasn't for us to be here, we would not be here. No man on this earth can get rid of us, so the white man is fooling himself. If they did think they got rid of us, they have demolished nothing because I, a Native American, am still here. What the white man does not realize is that he must pay for everything he does when he meets the Creator. Every man, even a Native American, will pay when he meets the Creator. If you don't pay for it in this world, you will pay for it in the next, whether you believe or not—the dirt, the bloodshed, and the killing of the Native Americans on Turtle Island as well as the way Native peoples were mistreated. They actually think they will *never* pay for what they did. I guarantee if you don't pay for it in this world, you will pay for it in the next world, but they don't believe this. Sometimes, as a test, I do just a little dirt myself and get the bad back, and then I do good and get the good back. So this really exists, as I've been able to experiment with this idea myself.

You all should try this sometime. You will understand that it works and that you should not do bad things to other people. It is better to do it and to be aware than to do bad things to people and not be aware and wonder why bad things are happening to you. I am so glad I have the wisdom and knowledge to think of this. Just to do it on a small scale to see if it is really true. For those of you reading this book who don't believe it, just give it a try and you will find out it is very real. Most of us say we don't believe something, but we don't try it out to see if it is real. The same goes if we don't see something with our naked eye, then we don't think it exists. There are a whole lot of things that exist we don't know anything about. If we knew everything, we could tell you how much an ant weighs and a fly weighs.

I am open to learning everything because I know there is a lot on this earth that I don't know. There are other men on this earth who know things

I don't know. I do pray to the Creator to guide me and to give me knowledge. Very seldom might this knowledge come from man. Sometimes when I hear a baby cry, I get a message from the cry. Sometimes when I see kids playing, I receive knowledge just watching and hearing them play. Also, I pick up knowledge from the fishes of the sea, the birds in the air, the bears, the deer, the buffalo, the eagle, and the reptiles. I get knowledge from all these different species and learn something from every one of them.

I am a very observant indigenous person. I am a little bit different from everybody, as that is how the Creator made me. I am so glad I am different. I like taking the bones of a buffalo and making different types of whistles and jewelry. The bones from a deer make beautiful beads and necklaces. The bones from an eagle make a beautiful sound like that coming from the heavens. From the center of a fish bone, you can make different types of necklaces. So you see, we should not abuse all these different species. We are not like the Europeans; we had a purpose and reason to use these species and not to kill them for sport. The older generation of indigenous peoples used to make many different things out of these species. I've never made anything out of eagle bones, but I am almost sure I can. It is in indigenous people's makeup, and that is just the way the Creator made us.

It is up to us to use this knowledge and carry on the culture. The beauty of the whole thing is you know who you are. The Creator showed you who you are, and nobody can take that away from you. At least intelligent people recognize who we are as indigenous peoples. They can identify me with a race of people, but I cannot identify them with any race of people. When the Great Spirit can show you who you are, anybody can identify you because it is real and not something phony. It is not like you went in the closet and put on Indian clothing. The Great Spirit chose you, and you can tell the difference when one is chosen and when one is an imitator. One looks original and was chosen by the Creator, and the one who went into the closet and put on the clothes is a phony. You can tell the difference, and believe me, I know the difference between something made in China and something made on the reservation by a Native American. It has a different feel and a different look. There are always people trying to imitate us, but it can never be the same. The Creator put that great gift into our hands, not anyone else. These gifts include making carvings, jewelry, totem poles, and gems; silversmithing; painting; and sculpture. You can tell the difference in the Native works. I am very proud of who I am as a Native of Turtle Island.

One day we will have our land back, and nobody will ever be able to interfere with our lives again. We weren't savage; we never took over anyone's land. All this madness, killing us and taking over our land—they are the savages. Believe me, the Creator is going to have something for them. One day everything is going to change in the blink of an eye. They are going to be on the bottom, and we are going to be on the top. The best thing is that we are not going to take anything from anybody. We are just taking back what is ours. We will be the rulers and judge everything like before the Europeans came to Turtle Island. But we will be just to every man according to his deeds. We will not be unjust to anyone, no matter their race, color, or creed. We are not going to treat the Europeans they way they treated us. We will be just to everyone, no matter who they are. That doesn't sound like a savage to me!

The Europeans put all the bad deeds they do onto other people. It's never them committing wrongful acts, even though they come onto our lands. The spirit will lead us on how to govern the earth; we will not go by our instinct or what we think. So you see, I know it is better to go by the higher spirit. I have already seen in a vision that we are getting Turtle Island back and will be led by the spirit. What a great day that is going to be. I will be back to what I once used to be, and there won't be any back-biting, jealousy, or lying because the Creator is going to govern this time, and we are going to be his servants. There will be no trickery or nonsense. It is going to be a different day and time. What a great day that is going to be! By that time I will be using all my twelve senses, plus my inner eye.

You know at one time we as indigenous people could speak every language on the face of the earth; we had that gift. You know there was nothing slow and out-of-date about the Native American people before the Europeans came. But the biggest problem I have with people is when I tell them I am an Indian and they think I don't want to be black. I look black and know my color has not changed. But the biggest thing I found is that most do not know what the real indigenous people look like—they don't even know who they are or where they come from. I also discovered that the those who I thought were knowledgeable about the Native peoples are not. The late Chief Mayo always told me that, but I never paid it any attention until he went over to the other side and I found this to be true. When they say the black people lost their identity, culture, and traditional way of life, that is very true.

Every race of people comes in different nationalities, and because you are black and they are black, then you are the same nationality. But that is not so. The biggest problem I have with most people identifying me with them is that they think we are all the same. We are all mixed up with one another, and some of us came from Africa. Before the Europeans came here, the original Natives were dark complexioned just like the African was, and we are all mixed and got everybody confused. The European, he writes the books, and with the computers and everything, he wants us to think all Native Americans have a type of Asian look. The ones with the Asian look have been mixed with other peoples and live on the West Coast. We on the East Coast mixed mostly with the Europeans. But I am going to give you something to think about. Everyone was black on this planet at one time before the European set foot here, but we were different nationalities—for example, Egyptians, Ethiopians, and Zulus were all of the black race. The thing about me is that I was never taught by man but by the Creator, and that is how I know who I am. How you know who you are is when you are told by the Creator, not by man.

My grandmother planted the seed about my Native American roots, and I found out the rest. Nobody had to tell me; it was the Creator who led me to my ancestors. The Creator led me to the Cherokee, but I never knew about the Montauk until later, and the Creator led me there too. But the problem is that you can have trouble with the Indians already there.

By coming in later and just finding out your roots, they tell you these are not your people. The Creator spoke to me one night and told me if I am not the same Banks, they are not the same people they found with the same last names. You know I am not making this up, as I get my information from the Creator. I am a very spiritual man, and nothing I am telling you comes from man. This is why I know it is accurate because it is coming straight from heaven, *not* from earth. Some of us were born here on earth to bring back the knowledge of what our people were stripped of. I am one of the chosen ones who will bring back what our peoples once lost.

Whether people will not accept my last name and reject me from who I am, it is not going to change a thing because I am who I am. I still think Native and dress Native, and I will not cut my hair, no matter what, because our long hair is our strength, and we are not supposed to cut it. This is part of the covenant: we are not supposed to cut our hair because it shows who we are. I love my ponytail with the Buffalo silver nickels braided into it down my back. The Creator sends me ideas straight from the heavens. That is why when people see me, they ask where I get the fancy silver I wear down my ponytail. I tell them it comes from the heavens, straight from the Creator. To me, the Creator is the highest spirit; he is the one who gives you ideas that you have to pay attention to. The Creator also gives you all the answers, but you have to ask him first. You don't have to believe because you know he will do it. It is the Christians who say you have to believe, but we as Native Americans don't believe; we know he is going to do it.

The biggest problem I have with people is their concern about my complexion. My biggest wish is to keep the Native traditions alive: eating venison, buffalo, fish, corn, and squash, which is our food; wearing the buckskin and ribbon shirts and the breastplates and moccasins; not cutting our long hair; and honoring our ancestors through the powwow's Grand Entry. In other words, living like a Native every day and not as a one-day Indian when we have powwows. There is a big difference between being chosen by the Creator and going into the closet to put on Native clothes for just one day. I will always keep the tradition alive until the day I die. I will never lose it because I know where it comes from, as I made an oath with the Creator. If I was the only one on this planet to carry on the traditions, then I would because I know where my help comes from. I do not care about other people's opinions about me. Once you find out who you are, it doesn't make any difference who you used to be.

The funny thing about New York is that once you are here and stay for a while, no matter where else you go, you want to come back to it. When I first came, I wanted to go back to Atlanta that same night because I had never seen so much garbage. A friend of mine was into music, and I was looking for him. One day I happened to be walking up Lenox Avenue to 126th Street. As I passed the Chinese restaurant, I ran into my friend who was eating oxtail, rice, and toast. I'd been looking for him for about a month. I had been walking up and down Harlem and had finally found him. Because he traveled a lot, I started going with him to Chicago, Detroit, Milwaukee, Los Angeles, Saint Louis, Cincinnati, Cleveland, and more. We would stay in a hotel for two to three days and then return to New York. I was still staying with my aunt until her husband told me to get my own place. After traveling with my musician friend who played the trumpet, clarinet, drums, and saxophone, I realized New York is the best city.

Before I left Atlanta, I thought it was the best place in the world; it was known as the cream of the crop. New York is the best because you can live a country life, a suburb life, and a city life. Plus, you are exposed to more stuff in New York than anywhere else in the world. New York brings out the best in you; I never knew I was so talented until I came here. I didn't have any sense when I was down South. I just wished some of my buddies who were such good artists like me had come up here. They turned into drunks because they stayed in Atlanta and all they did was work and go home. They were never exposed to culture like I was in New York. There are no art schools in Atlanta like there are in New York City, but if there were, their lives would have been different, and their talents would have been made known, like mine. I went home to Atlanta in the sixties to see my family, and when I stayed two days longer, my dad packed my bags himself, took my ass to the train station, and made sure I returned to New

York. He could see the positive and big change in me that he never saw in Atlanta. As the train pulled away, my father smiled, waved bye-bye, and hugged my mother; he was so happy I was on my way to New York. After this visit home, the whole family never saw me again for a long time, about twelve to fifteen years. They were glad I had left home because if I had remained in Atlanta, I would not be where I am today.

I realized they were right because I had a friend in Long Island, an island-born Native, who told me I learned some sense when I came to New York and met them. She (a Cherokee) said I had no sense in Georgia, "But now you have sense since you met us." She was a very good friend and used to come to Manhattan to see me and attend Abyssinia Baptist Church. Between her and Miss Ruth, they acted like fortune-tellers who knew it was right that I came to New York. Even a fortune-teller in Africa told me New York was my town. If some of my buddies in Atlanta had left to go to a big city like Detroit, they would not have become drunks because they would have been exposed to more, and their talents would have been realized. The system in the South is set to make sure you become either dead, a drunk, or in jail, and if I had stayed in Atlanta, that would have been my fate. I know the best move I made in my life was when I came North. Now I know what I truly became, exactly who I am, and what I'm supposed to be doing in life.

Now when I go back down South, they want to know how I got all this information to prove we are really Native Americans, how I found the family's roots. They want to know how I got to the point of doing the sculptures and other artworks. They knew I could draw when I left the South, but it was not as enriched as my oil paintings. Even my sisters say that my skin tone changed to a dark reddish brown and that my vocabulary, voice, actions, and ways have become northern expressions instead of the southern expressions I had when we were kids. They see a total difference in my character, and my personality is definitely not the same. I will never forget when my teacher Miss Banks said traveling is an education. I never dreamed in my life I would be wearing a war bonnet or that somebody would pass a war bonnet on to me and ask me to take his place. You never know what the Creator has in store for you. But I do know you must do whatever you have to do, even though there are people who will try to stop you. You must do what the Creator wants you to do. He is the guide I listen to as the higher spirit, since man is jealous. They tell lies on you, but the truth always overpowers the lies. The funny thing is, to be a Native American, it ain't who you know, it ain't what you know, and it ain't who you look like. It is what you got as proof that you are Native American.

I try to go the Gathering of Nations powwow in Albuquerque, New Mexico, every year. My main thing is marching in the Grand Entry to honor my ancestors. Everything else is commercial, a money thing. After I participate in the Grand Entry, I just walk around and watch the competition dancing, talk with some of my friends, and see what I can purchase from some of the Navajo and Pueblo peoples, especially the turquoise jewelry, ribbon shirts, headbands, Apache silver, and Cherokee moccasins. I find myself spending two to three hundred dollars, even though as an artist I can pretty much make some of this stuff myself. I purchase their items to show appreciation and to learn from their artwork. We artists learn from one another, just as a writer learns from another writer, a singer learns from another singer, and a musician learns from another musician. So you see, each one teaches someone else. In April 2013 Professor Morehand-Olufade and I attended the Gathering of the Nations Powwow, and she was stunned to see the thousands of Native Americans from all over America gathered together in the open-air stadium in Albuquerque. When I went to the desk to sign up as a participant in the "Grand Entry" ceremony, which is about the honoring of our ancestors, a young woman shouted at me, "Welcome, Chief," and I was not even wearing my war bonnet. During the lineup of the Grand Entry participants, I was placed in the front of the line to lead everyone onto the field at the start of the ceremony. As usual, I participated in several of the ceremonial dances that also honor our Native American ancestry.

I admire the singer/songwriter Smokey Robinson because he is very talented and God gave him so many gifts. He knows he was put on earth to share his talents. He's written so many songs and never bragged about it.

He was never the jealous type, and when he saw talent in others, he always brought them up and helped them. I liked all his songs, but the best one is "I Don't Care What People Think about Me." He knows his mission on earth and the gifts God gave him, and that is why he doesn't care about what people think about him. He did what God told him to do for all. The things he does remind me of myself. I am willing to help anybody in the art field who does the same things I do, such as sculpting, oil painting, carving, poetry, and carpentry. I know my mission on earth too, and God gave me these gifts so that I could share them with others. I will continue sharing with others. I will continue doing what I am supposed to do, no matter how much other people are jealous of me or lie on me. I don't care.

A funny thing about me that makes me different from other people is that when they share what they have, they think somebody is taking something from them. The Creator did not bless us with all this talent to keep it to ourselves. We are supposed to share with other artists who are trying to make it, but we as artists are not always doing this. The best thing about this is the more you share with other people, the more the Creator will bless you. I am going to keep doing what I am doing and share with others what the Creator blessed me with. One thing I cannot understand about people is that they don't come to you and ask that you teach them what you know. There are some artists out there who don't want to show you anything, even if you ask them, but I am not one of them. I have a good attitude and take my artwork very seriously. I could have been one of the people not born with talent and needing to ask other artists for information, and they could have bad attitudes. I have seen other artists show bad attitudes and who don't want to share what they know because they fear this will take something from them. They should know that when they do share their knowledge, the Creator will double their blessings. Some people are born with a gift, and others have to be taught. I was born with the gift of drawing. When people see you as a child with a gift, they never tell you that the gift is from the Creator. I don't know whether they don't know or are just jealous. I was in my sixties before I found out my drawing ability was a gift from the Creator. I was in my seventies before I realized the spirit talks to you and gives you all the answers. So you see, man never told me that my gift is from the Creator or that the Creator would give me all the answers. I was seventy years old before the Holy Spirit gave me the answers.

Everything I have gained in life never came from man. Maybe they don't realize it themselves, and just seeing me do my artwork, they don't know where my gift comes from. I was in my sixties and seventies before I realized its origin. So many people look at me and say, "Boy! You are smart," and I tell them right away it is not me but the Creator in me giving me all the answers. I am not going to fault man for not telling me this because I just found this out myself at the age of sixty and seventy. It ain't what you didn't know; it is what you know now. I didn't realize that this was my blessing of being an artist, but now I do! I will take it seriously and share what I have with anyone. I will keep praying and asking the Creator to guide me in all I do for the rest of my life. I try not to be like the rest of the people who have a gift and don't share it with others. I strongly believe that the more you share, the more the Creator will give you. Most people don't believe this, and that is why they don't share. My opinion is mine, and their opinion is theirs. However, it is fact that the more you share, the more you get.

I am trying to figure out how I am going to make it, as I hurt my back and head in 2008. As I started writing this book in 2011, I woke up one morning and could not even walk. My nerve is sitting on my spine and has paralyzed my right leg. Because I'm an energetic guy, sometimes I wonder why the Creator let this happen to me. Each day when I get up and look in the mirror, I can't believe the Creator let this happen to me, and I wonder why. I have a good nature. I take every medication for it. I had two injections in my back and need to wear braces in my shoes. Nothing is doing me any good, and now they claim an operation would take the nerve off my spine. I can either walk partly crippled, or I can be sitting in a wheelchair for the rest of my life after having surgery. So I will keep taking therapy, wearing braces, and hoping the Creator will bring me back to my natural state.

My mother is still living at the age of one hundred, and she can walk, run, and jump. I am very proud of her. The cutest thing happened: my oldest sister, my brother, and I, we all fell, and we're all on a damn cane and taking the same medication. I am in New York, they are in Atlanta, and we all have the same problem. Thank God my mother is okay and never had to use a cane. I don't know if the Creator is trying to show us all something, given that we are having the same problem at the same time and in the same year. I am in terrible pain as I write this book, but I truly believe that by the time it is published, I will be back to my normal ways. The doctors are trying to help me, but I think I have to go to a reservation to see an Indian medicine man. First, I will pray to the Creator to show me what I can do for myself. He might send me to a medicine man. We Natives have everything in the world to cure anything, and this just dawned on me, as going to these modern doctors is not helping me. Now I know to pray to the Creator for help to send me to my Native peoples or to show me what to do for myself. The modern ways are not helping, and the next step is to the reservation. My leg needs to be blessed with eagle feathers. I know this works because when my baby son was complaining he had worms in his head, we took him from doctor to doctor, but he never got better. When he was blessed with the eagle feathers, he never felt it again. I know the same thing will help me when I get blessed with the eagle feathers on the reservation, and then I will walk naturally again. Even just talking about how I will heal makes me feel better, simply by saying the words. I will keep eating my buffalo venison and taking herbs while I wait to hear from the Creator.

I am a Cherokee, Muscogee Creek, and Montauk Indian, and I love wearing my cowboy boots. I have not been able to wear them since the accident, but I put them on the other day for the first time. Boy, did I feel good! I did not go outside with them but walked around the house instead. It felt good to be able to put them on again. As Native people, we like to wear our cowboy boots when we are not at ceremonies and powwows, during which we wear moccasins. I hope in April 2013 when we attend the powwow in Albuquerque that I will be able to wear my cowboy boots. Life is all about seeing yourself being better and doing better. I already saw myself in my cowboy boots walking like I used to walk. If I don't see myself going to Albuquerque and Phoenix before it happens, it will never take place. Your mind travels first, and your behind follows.

I realized the other day there must be a Creator. The spirit started talking to me one Sunday morning and said, "I gave you art and showed you how to sculpt. I gave you poetry and even showed you are indigenous to this country. I also gave you your name, Eagle Eye Bear Claw Black, Brown, Red, Yellow, and White Buffalo." I next heard a voice clear as day tell me, "Now you know I exist, and all men who do great things know where their talents come from. You are a great artist because your ability comes from me. I am the most high, the Creator, and all that you know comes from me. I am the one who works through you *as you*. I am the most high power and the Creator of all men who do great things. I chose you to do what you do. Any time you see a good singer or teacher, remember it is me making them great. Not them, but me! I am giving you the ability to see where your blessings come from and where others get theirs. It is through me, the most high source, the Creator."

After I made my prayer and he brought this vision to me that morning, I will forever make my prayer thanking the Creator for giving me this gift here on earth until I return to paradise where I come from. I remember when I was a little boy of about seven years old, I asked my grandmother how you know when God is talking to you. She told me I have to have direct experience with the Creator myself. At seventy years old, I finally had the experience the first time on Sunday morning, November 6, 2011. Thanks be to the Creator! Mama is dead and gone, and the spirit finally came to me. What a beautiful feeling it is when you know who you are, what you are supposed to be doing, and why you are here, and the high spirit shows it all to you. This is why I know he exists because what I got man did not give to me, and he sure cannot take it from me. What I am telling you is there is a high spirit above looking down on earth. There is not a one of us to whom he did not give some type of talent. To some of us he gave the gift of singing, science, teaching, mathematics, music, art, doctoring, architecture, building, healing—I can go on and on. There is not a one of us whom the Creator has not given some type of gift or talent. The gifts I know that I have are art, money, poetry, numbers, and building, and this I can say proudly.

I remember when I was a carpenter working on the East River doing dock work on that particular site. I was bending over, looking at the water of the East River, and I fell in. Nobody noticed I was down in the river looking up at them, and nobody could see me. I was fully clothed. Thank God I used to hang out with the big boys when I was five years old and learned how to swim. Otherwise, I would have drowned in the East River. When I came up out of the water and joined the rest of the guys, they asked me, "What happened to you?" I told them I lost my balance and fell into the water. I'm glad as a kid my mother never tried to hold me down; she always said she felt I could protect myself, but not my brother and sisters. The time I fell in the East River, I thought about when I used to run with the older guys and how I once nearly drowned at seven years old. One of them saved me from drowning in twenty-five feet of water. I slid behind them to the diving board and started sinking, and my little behind was picked up and put on the side by a seventeen-year-old who spotted me. I can thank God for my life today that he spared me; otherwise, I would not be here to write this book. That young man saved my life.

All the experiences I had as a child of seven and eight running around with guys in high school when I was in the third grade made me the man I am today. I noticed one thing when I lived in the Gray Street Projects in Atlanta: everybody was the same, equal. If you asked for a cigarette, you would be given one, no questions asked. Nobody thought you were too young to do anything. I used to play cards—whist, blackjack, spades, and strip poker—at the age of five with grown men at the community porch where everybody could hang out and sit down to play cards and such. Nobody ever said, "Little boy, go home." Everybody—dad, mama, and children—were the damn same and equal. The funny thing is, I have learned nothing new in life except my Native American heritage. I already had experience with life itself. Now that I am older, I want to do two big eight-foot sculptures for the Poospatuck Reservation if they ever give me permission. I always was an artist, but I came into my artistic abilities as I grew. I always wanted to study medicine because some of my friends became medical doctors, dentists, lawyers, district attorneys, policemen, and judges, and I always looked at them as being much smarter than me. I could never stand to see a blank piece of paper unless I drew something on it. As I matured, I realized that each and every one of us has a different talent, and that art is my talent, no matter which way I swing the bat.

Since I found my identity about being a true Native American and I do sculpture, wood carving, and oil painting, I now feel good about my artistic abilities, and I don't look at my former friends as being more brilliant than me. One thing I like over in Europe is that they respect art and artists and the different talents people have, unlike down South in the United States. You have a lot of good artists down South, but they don't respect art down there and the gifts the Creator gave them. I went to school with two brothers who were excellent artists, but they became drunks, and no one would ever want to see them. All this happens because of a lack of exposure to art, and teachers don't motivate them to be artistically creative and show their abilities. When I have the chance to go to Atlanta and see the two brothers, I will give them paper and pencils to see if they still have their artistic abilities—for example, drawing horses running in different directions. I read in the Cherokee books that Cherokee Indians always did carving, painting, sculpting, and basket weaving and made jewelry and pottery. I am definitely a Cherokee because I spend all my time doing the same things I read in the Cherokee books. Now that I know my mission on earth, I will continue doing all that I am doing.

What I really want to do is go out to the Cherokee Reservation in Oklahoma and see if I could do my sculpture there, or my oil paintings, or even build teepees or houses (as a retired carpenter) on Native American reservations. I feel bad about having the gifts that the Creator wants me to do for my peoples, and I am being denied by other tribal Indians who ignore me because I am not from their tribes. Before I talk too fast, I don't know how the Cherokee peoples are going to act toward me because my skin is dark, even though the dark-skinned Indians are the originals. There is so much division among Native peoples themselves. It was easy for the Europeans to take over from the fifteen hundred up until now. The biggest trouble I found is that the Natives started looking at it from a color thing after the Europeans came over here. Then the divisions came about between the dark-skinned and the fair-skinned Indians all over the country. Now you see white people saying they are Natives of this country. If the Natives had ever looked like white people, they would not have been surprised to see Europeans when they came over here. The Natives had never seen pale-skinned people before. What I do know is that the Europeans started the divisions by saying anyone with dark skin is from Africa, and if your skin is fair, you are from Asia. Let us get this shit straight. The Native Americans are not from Africa or Asia. My grandmother always told me we are from right here and nowhere else. The Creator already revealed it to me that the Natives don't come from anywhere else, and we are definitely from right here. Now whom should I believe, the Creator and what he revealed to me or what the white man has written in books? Do I have a choice? Yes. I think I'd rather go along with what the Creator revealed to me because he made all of us.

So you see, by making my prayer five times a day to the Creator and writing Chinese, Arabic, and Hebrew in a prayer for the last thirty years, never skipping a day, many things have been revealed to me. I write the Lord's Prayer in Chinese and Hebrew, and I write the prayer of Allah in Arabic every day. With that type of consistency, you can look for the Creator to reveal anything to you. I did not go to school to write these prayers in Chinese, Arabic, and Hebrew. This was revealed to me by the Creator. I started writing these three prayers in less than a week at the same time. I am going to give you a tip. When you know that man didn't give you something but that the Creator did, you appreciate it. I used to say it was me until I realized I could never have done this myself; it was the Creator who showed me. Since I've had this experience with the three different languages and prayers, I am asking the Creator as a Cherokee person to lead me to my Cherokee roots. I want the Creator to reveal to me how to read, write, and speak Cherokee, Navajo, Apache, Shinnecock, Unkechaug, and Montauk. I also want the Creator to let me know I belong to the Montauk, the Shinnecock, or the Unkechaugs. One thing about the Creator is that he reveals things when you least expect it, and all I have to do is keep writing, keep praying, and keep having faith. I know one day he will lead me to the rest of my people on my father's side, the Banks.

Kwadwo, my eldest son, and I traveled to Miami, Florida, in 1986 when he was four years old to attend a religious meeting. The main person was called Yaweh, and people thought he was a God-saving person who would save mankind. This was the first time I ate unleavened bread. I remember he got up and asked how many people would like to rise on unleavened bread instead of regular bread. I thought it was good idea. When we were sitting in the cafeteria eating unleavened bread, fish, beef, rice, corn, and green vegetables, my son would not eat anything. A nice-looking lady about thirty years old who was from Florida told me I should not let Kwadwo eat any food that would affect his brain. My son was not an eater, but his maternal grandmother told me when we came back to New York that I should not worry about this, as the less food kids ate, the better their brains would be. She was right because Kwadjo was very bright and always did well in school for a little boy. Today he teaches and acts and is a graduate of Saint Lawrence University. He never ate a lot of food as a young child, and he still is not a big eater. My other son, Ali, is a big eater and always has been since he was a little kid. He is also very bright. So, is it the food, or is it the person? I would say it is the person because I am what I eat, but my sons are not what they eat. Just like we got different fingerprints, we all are different in many ways.

A funny thing: we were at another meeting one day, and there was such food as goat, lamb, fish, and chicken, and I just happened to mention how shrimp and red salmon are good for my brain. For God's sake, don't speak about Beluga caviar (from the black sturgeon fish) with sour cream on it. These foods really soup my brain up and make me extremely smart. I now understand why the guy kept asking Jesus questions about

93

what should he do, and Jesus kept telling him to go study himself. Even before I realized this, I had studied myself. We have to listen to the spirit within us, as it will give us all the answers. No matter what your mother, sister, or father thinks, the Creator makes each person. Even though you come through your mother and father, you are a separate individual. For God's sake, forget about what your so-called friends think about you. It is the Creator who made you, not man! You are trying to please the Creator. Most people try to please man and not the Creator. To give you a good example, most people look at me strangely because they've never seen a dark-skinned Indian. If I was not listening to the Creator who pointed out who I am, and because they look at me so strangely, I would be acting like them and calling myself an African American like them. The Creator already pointed out who I am, which is an indigenous of this land, Turtle Island, which the Europeans named America. You don't get this information from your mother, father, sister, brother, or outsider; it comes straight from the Creator. Sometimes when I am walking in the street, people look at me so strangely because I look so different. It used to bother me, but now I don't give a damn because if I was down on my knees, not one of them would come and help me. As a matter of fact, if I was down, they would be glad. They would say, "Look at that old nigger going around saying he is an Indian but look at him now! This is good." This is what they would say if it happened, but it would never happen, my man.

The Great Spirit always takes care of his people. From the time I was born, I was always very independent. My own mother and father knew I was different from the time I came on this earth. I feel good to be who I am, knowing who I am and knowing the Creator connected me back to my great ancestors. The Europeans thought they had cut us off from our bloodline, but I was chosen to bring it back. Sometimes I cannot believe it myself. I never dreamed I would be appointed for this mission. Everybody is called for different things, and I might as well accept it. Oh boy, you should see how some of these so-called want-to-be Indians look at me. First of all, they are looking at my dark skin, and they all can go to hell! When I think about who gave me this assignment, I couldn't care less about what they think. I found out people in America have a problem with skin color. They believe you have to be a certain color to belong to a certain group, but the Creator proved to me this is not true. Don't get me wrong, I thought the same way until my grandmother told me we were Indians and the Creator showed me. When I was a little boy, I asked my grandmother how you know if the spirit is telling you things. She said I will know when it happens. Now I know. One thing I do know, when you come in contact with the Creator and don't know what your assignment is going to be, he will let you know. I didn't know there was an assignment to go along with being in contact with the Creator. I used to wonder how preachers became preachers, and then I realized they came in contact with the Creator and learned their assignments. I also used to wonder how doctors became doctors, engineers became engineers, and scientists became scientists. I always wanted to be one of them, or even an actor, but it never came to be.

I didn't realize that was not my assignment, and those reading this book must know that each person has his or her individual assignment in life. Yesterday I went down to the art school and a student named Donna told me the whole school talked about how they had never seen anyone do sculptures as fast I can. Why can I do this? Because it is my assignment: sculpture, oil painting, and carpentry. I did everything else before this, but it never worked. Man can never tell you your assignment; only the Creator can tell you who you are. This is the only way you are going to find out, my man! When you see all these great people doing things, it is because they already know their assignments, and that is why they do things so well. So for those of you reading this book, if things you are doing are not working for you, you've got to wait on the Creator to show you your assignments. This ain't nothing you have to pray about. God just gave it to me, and in due time he will give it to you, no matter how old you are. I got my assignment in my fifties. Even though I got my assignment directly from God, you have to listen to the Creator and not to man because most people don't know their assignments unless they are spiritual. And quit looking at other people and wishing you were like them because your assignment could be better than theirs. Most people say, "I wish I could sing like him, I wish I could write like him, I wish I could do math like him, I wish I could live in a big house like him, I wish I could drive a car like him." We live in a material world, and everybody seems to want what the other fellow has instead of looking at what the Creator gave each one of us.

There ain't a person on earth to whom the Creator did not give a gift. I can talk now because I found out what my gift was at a late age and that God gave everyone a gift. I used to look at the great basketball players, like Wilt Chamberlain, and the football players, like Jim Brown, and the singers, like Jackie Wilson, and watch the science channel and see all these great men. I wondered what my gift was, and in 2000 I discovered it when I met the Shinnecock. It never is too late to find out one's gift, and you're never too old to learn. When I met the Shinnecock, they did not point out my gift to me; it just automatically came to me a couple of months later. I was so interested in Indians when I saw them, and the first thing that came into my mind was, "Oh! I can draw black Indians," and I got very interested in doing artworks of Indians.

I went to a gathering of all Native American tribes in Washington, DC, and I remember seeing Natives in all shades, styles, and complexions. I also remember a dark-complexioned Native American from Oklahoma who said I am a chief but not her chief. My spirit told me then she did not want to respect anyone dark like me being a chief regardless of where the person came from, even though she was also dark complexioned. Indians always have a problem with me, and I don't know whether it is jealousy or what. With her attitude, she needs to do more traveling. She's obviously never been to the Poospatuck, Shinnecock, Narragansett, or Pequot Reservations, where those Native Americans are dark complexioned, and has only been between Oklahoma and Washington, D.C. Being Native American doesn't go by your color; it goes by your spirit and what the Creator puts in you. It tells me by the derogatory statement she made that she is dealing with color, and even though she looks Native, she has no Native spirit within her. Like it was a big deal because she was from

Oklahoma and my ancestors were led from Georgia to Oklahoma, but I was born in Georgia. It was the same Trail of Tears, and that could have been why she might have been born in Oklahoma. I did not ask where she was born because I did not care. After my run-in with this woman, the rest of the day was nice. Guest speakers talked about the Treaty of 1866 that stated what we were supposed to receive but never got. We went there demanding what we should have been given, and we are still demanding it up to this day in the year 2012. The key to everything is not to give up, and I truly believe one day something big will happen, and we will have our land back. The second time we went to Washington, DC, we went on the Longest Walk to remind us of how our ancestors walked from Georgia to Oklahoma on the Trail of Tears.

Before my last trip to Washington, DC, I met my cousin Angela Molette and her mother, Barbara Finley, who live in Enid, Oklahoma. They have a Native American museum and heritage center in Enid. I sent them more than twenty paintings to put in their museum, along with two carvings. I also gave them a large painting of an ex-girlfriend and me that you see immediately when you walk in the museum's door. I have only been to their museum one time, in 2007, and did not get a chance to stay long. I drove to Oklahoma with some people from New York, but they acted out, and we had to leave Enid abruptly because of their behavior. This is all right, as I understand some people's behavior, and I left that behind. I am planning to go back out there pretty soon because I never got a chance to sit down and talk with my cousins. But I do talk with them on the phone here and there. I also have relatives in Tulsa, Oklahoma, but I never had a chance to go there. I met a guy in a gas station in Oklahoma, and he asked me if I was from a certain area around Tulsa. I told him I am from New York. He said that I resemble some people from there, and I asked their name, and he said Banks, which is my name. He told me I look just like the Banks family of Tulsa, Oklahoma. During that time I was on my way to Enid and made arrangements to meet him on a specific day when I would be heading back to New York so that he could take me to meet the Banks family in Tulsa, who are Indian. One day I will make a special trip to find the Banks family in Tulsa. If I find them, I would like to do a great sculpture as a landmark out there. In the future, I want to go all over different cities in America and do paintings and sculptures of Native Americans. I truly believe this is my calling. We all have a calling, and this is mine. I hope one day this will happen, and I am waiting to get permission to do it. Anyone who wants me to do a sculpture or a painting of just Native Americans on or off the reservation, as long as it is Native peoples, I am willing to do it.

Studying Islam and talking to Elijah Muhammad, who said we must have some of this land we can call our own, sort of woke me up, and I said, "Wait a minute. My ancestors owned a lot of land, and they've still got it." This is the reason why I want to look into this to see if there is something I can call my own and pass down to my children too. After coming north to New York, I got a little wiser. This is why I want to research my family more than ever. The rest of my family is not interested, so I have to do this on my own. They don't want to meet the new people of our family who have done research. All they are interested in is themselves. I have another cousin by the name of Donnell Shinholster; his mother and my father were sister and brother. He is also interested in family research, and we both have studied Islam. The following pages detail our genealogy research.

The Paternal Family Genealogy of Robert Banks Cornelius Jr., or Eagle Eye Bear Claw Black, Brown, Red, Yellow, and White Buffalo

—— ✺ ——

WHEN I, PROFESSOR Darnell A. Morehand-Olufade, chose to coauthor Robert Banks Cornelius, Jr.'s autobiography. The first thing he said to me was, "I want to know who are my people and where did they come from?" He always knew who he was, but his family history remained somewhat of a mystery. After starting to do serious genealogical research, he found it truly fascinating to actually discover the authentic records and photographs of his descendants pertaining to the Blackburn, Hudson, Childers, Ashley, and Banks families. In the following statement, Robert shares his sincere opinion on his paternal family's heritage and also believes a television miniseries should be developed and presented to the world about the interactions during the 1700s, 1800s, and 1900s among his white, Native American, and black ancestors:

I was amazed when I found my fourth-generation great-grandfather, Burrell Vaudry Hudson, and a photograph of him. The greatest feelings I have is that every time I go to the mirror, I know I look just like him. The only difference is that my face is black and his was white. No matter which way I comb my hair, I look exactly like him. I know that I came from him and am very proud I look exactly like him. The feeling I have is very hard to describe, and it makes me feel real good to know who I came from. These white people were really married into my family and proved my roots are white.

I feel proud of it, and why is because I can't do nothing about it. I did not choose my family. I was born into my family.

Robert Banks Cornelius Jr.'s two cousins, Elaine Collins (first cousin) and Reverend Vivian Thomas-Breitfield (second cousin), had started the family's genealogical research thirty years ago and found original microfiche documents of the Lewis Blackburn family, who were connected to the Cherokee Indian removal, also known as the Trail of Tears, from New Echota, Calhoun, Georgia, to Chelsea, Oklahoma, in 1838. Elaine and Viviane's genealogy research findings were remarkable and extremely significant to the continuation of the research Robert and I started in 2010. Another cousin, William Banks, contributed to the family genealogy research by giving us a printed Banks's family tree that specifically showed the names and dates of birth, starting when Robert was born on December 16, 1940, and backward to Harry Banks, Robert's great-grandfather, third generation, who was born in 1836.

It was in the same year (2010) that I became a member of Ancestry. com for the second time and created a family tree for Robert Banks Cornelius Jr. Everyone who has started genealogy research on their family knows a family tree is first created with your name at the bottom of the tree. Then the person enters the name of his or her parents and ancestors into the boxes on the different levels, as shown in the example of Robert's paternal family tree that is available for the public to view on the Ancestry.com website. The experience we had researching and discovering Robert's genealogy (paternal) roots was like putting together a giant puzzle, and the puzzle pieces were all the documents, photographs, biographical information, and newspaper articles we needed to complete it.

The Blackburn Family

—— ❦ ——

First, we started our research of the Lewis Blackburn family by actually driving from New York to the New Echota-Cherokee Capital State Historic Site in Calhoun, Georgia, on May 16, 2012. On May 18, Robert and I arrived at this site and requested permission to do genealogy research in the reference library. Mr. David Gomez, a security officer at the site, did not hesitate to take us into the library and led us immediately to a reference book that contained the names and historical information of the families who were "recorded as individual Cherokees in the United States official census of the Cherokee Nation conducted in 1835" (Tyner 1974, 56). I started to speed-read through the pages, searching for the names of Lewis Blackburn, Polly Blackburn, Frances Henrietta Blackburn Hudson, and Lewis B. Blackburn that were on the copy of the 1851 Siler Rolls that Robert's cousins Elaine and Vivianne had sent to him thirty years ago. In less than two minutes, I read that Lewis Blackburn was the head of household that contained the following persons, described as one half-breed and ten quarter-bloods. He also owned a mill, a ferryboat, and twenty-one slaves. There was one farmer and two people who could read English. The five weavers and spinners I take license to speculate were Native Americans.

The more I read, the more I realized there was certainly a wealth of historical genealogical information to be gleaned from primary source materials regarding the interrelationships of the Blackburn and Hudson families through marriage and their experiences as "white men who applied for residence in the Cherokee Nation in Georgia 1831" (Warren and Weeksorgia 1987). The aforementioned was a book that contained a list of 208 names of those who were granted a license to reside among the Cherokees after having filed the appropriate affidavits. I have taught American history for thirteen years and have been involved with genealogy research since 2005. After finding this exciting historical information, I became determined to continue requesting as many reference books as possible during our visit to the New Echota-Cherokee Capital State Historic Site. I made photocopies of numerous pages of the first reference book and turned my attention to the second book that was brought to me by the site librarian.

Upon skimming quickly through the second book, I suddenly shouted, forgetting I was in a library, for Robert to come and see what I had found. In the book titled *Unhallowed Intrusion: A History of Cherokee Families in Forsyth County, Georgia*, were the names Lewis Blackburn, Polly Blackburn, Frances Hudson, and Lewis Blackburn Hudson, who were considered to be "Cherokee descendants remaining in Georgia in 1851–52 and were enrolled from thirteen counties: Call (Bartow), Chatham, Cherokee, Cobb, DeKalb, Forsyth, Gilmer, Gordon, Gwinnett, Lumpkin, Murray Union and Walker" (Shadburn 1993, 712). What was more surprising, these same family members' names were found on the Siler Roll, including their personal identification numbers: #1665 Lewis Blackburn, age seventy-three; #1666 Polly Blackburn, wife, age sixty-six; #1667 Frances Hudson, daughter, age thirty-five; and #1668 Lewis Blackburn Hudson, grandson, age eleven. They were given different personal identification numbers when this same family was listed on the 1852 Chapman Roll of Cherokee County, Georgia (Pamela Blakenship, e-mail message to Robert Banks Cornelius, October 6, 1999).

Lewis Blackburn (1778–1852), like other notable white men who lived in Georgia from 1832 to 1838 and were described as Cherokee planters there, had intermarried with the Cherokee tribe. His first wife, Mary (née Daniel) Buffington (1786–1852), was the widow of tavern keeper Thomas Buffington. It was after the War of 1812 that Lewis Blackburn settled in Cherokee County, Georgia. His marriage to a widow laid claim to the property and assets Mary had inherited from her husband's death.

He also established what became known as improvements, including a ferry operation in Forsyth, a gristmill, and seven acres of land in Lumpkin County. Mary and Lewis Blackburn were the parents of seven daughters who were recorded as quarter-bloods because their mother was mixed-blood. While researching the Blackburn family, we did not find if or when Lewis and Mary separated or divorced. They both died in 1852, presumably in Georgia. What we found more interesting is that they were buried next to each other in the Blackburn Cemetery on Old Federal Road in Forsyth County, Georgia.

The reality and facts are very clear. This same Lewis Blackburn was living with Polly (née Vann) Blackburn, their daughter Frances Henrietta (née Blackburn) Hudson, and their grandson, Lewis Blackburn Hudson, as specifically shown on the afore-mentioned Siler and Chapman Rolls dated 1851 and 1852, respectively. We did not research the Vann family in any detail, but any historian who knows something about the Native American history of the southeastern states of North and South Carolina, Tennessee, and Georgia would recognize the prominent Vann family name. Polly Vann-Blackburn (1787–1852) was a full-blood Cherokee. She was rumored to be the Indian concubine of Lewis Blackburn, and some referred to her as his second wife. She was not buried next to Lewis Blackburn but was instead buried at Hightower, near the Etowah River, in Forsyth County, Georgia. Her grandson, Lewis Blackburn Hudson (1841–1923), testified before the Department of the Interior, Commission to the Five Civilized Tribes, Chelsea, I. T., on November 18, 1900, and proved he was the direct descendant of a full-blood Cherokee and entitled to citizenship rights and benefits of the Cherokee Nation in Oklahoma and Georgia. Frances Henrietta Blackburn-Hudson (1815–1875) was Lewis Blackburn Hudson's mother, and her first husband was Madison E. Hudson. She had only the one son, Lewis Blackburn Hudson, from her first husband, and after divorcing him married a Mr. Weil and bore many children from him. After Frances Weil (née Blackburn/Hudson) died, her first husband, Madison E. Hudson, took take care of her orphaned (Weil) children.

ancestry

Oklahoma and Indian Territory, Dawes Census Cards for Five Civilized
Tribes, 1898-1914

Name:	Lewis B Hudson
Gender:	Male
Age:	59
Father Name:	Madison Hudson
Mother Name:	Frances Weil
Census Card Number:	5466
Dawes Enrollment Number:	13093
Tribe:	Cherokee
Enrollment Category:	By Blood

Source Information:

 Ancestry.com. Oklahoma and Indian Territory, Dawes Census Cards for Five Civilized Tribes, 1898-1914 [database on-line]. Provo, UT, USA: Ancestry.com Operations Inc, 2014. Original data: Enrollment Cards for the Five Civilized Tribes, 1898-1914. (National Archives Microfilm Publication M1186, 93 rolls); Records of the Bureau of Indian Affairs, Record Group 75, National Archives, Washington, D.C.

Description:
This database contains the Native American citizenship enrollment cards, sometimes referred to as census cards, that were prepared by the Dawes Commission. These enrollment cards apply to the Five Civilized Tribes - the Cherokee, Chickasaw, Choctaw, Creek, and Seminole. This database also contains the Final Rolls, or lists of individuals approved by the Commission for citizenship, as well as an Index to the Final Rolls.

© 2015 Ancestry

LEWIS BLACKBURN HUDSON DAWES CENSUS CARD
FOR FIVE CIVILIZED TRIBES, 1898 TO 1914

The white men and women who had intermarried with the Cherokees before the Treaty of New Echota in 1835 and who were also removed during the Trail of Tears were permitted to make claims to the US government pertaining to their property and improvements that were lost and not sold. We found written proof of how the material and monetary wealth was maintained for the future generations of the Blackburn family and other families of white men who were or were not Cherokee by blood; it was divided as follows (Shadburn 1989, 152):

Three payments for $12,668.01 were made to him in 1837–38 by the national government for his combined claims, listed on the register of payments as follows:

Valuation Improvements	$6,419.25
Spoliation for rent	$3,404.76
Ferry valuation	$2,000.00
Valuation on Hightower	$590.00
Additional Valuation	$254.00

Lewis Blackburn and all the other wealthy white and Cherokee families within the aforementioned counties of Georgia owned slaves, but we did not find any record of the national government giving compensation for the loss of any slaves. We can only presume these slave owners had to bear such losses, and obviously, as history bears witness, their slaves were forced to move with their slave owners. The approximate number of Cherokees, both whites and full-bloods, who were involved with the removal from the New Echota Cherokee Nation Capital Historical Site in Calhoun, Georgia, to the Oklahoma Indian Territory in 1838 was five thousand and included in that number were an unrecorded number of African slaves. Robert Banks Cornelius Jr.'s paternal family roots are *not* descendants of the Blackburn family's African slaves.

Before we discuss the Hudson family genealogy in great detail, it is necessary to bring to your attention that through our in-depth research of the Blackburn family descendants at the New Echota Capital Historical Site in Calhoun, Georgia, we also saw the name of Alfred Hudson listed as a white Georgia planter among the Cherokees from 1835 to 1838. At the time we discovered his name, we did not know anything about the Hudson family, but as the years went by and our genealogy research became more extensive, we worked backward to link Alfred Hudson as a neighbor of Lewis Blackburn before the removal from Georgia to Oklahoma. William Hudson (~1715–1790) was the father of Obediah Hudson (1735–1823), and Obediah Hudson was the father of Alfred Hudson (1801–1862). As you read the genealogy details in the following pages, you will see that all three men are direct descendants of Richard Hudson II, who was born in 1634 in Accomack, Virginia, and Robert Hudson I, who was born in Henrico County, Virginia, in 1662 and died in 1734 in Chesterfield County, Virginia. William Hudson was one of Robert Hudson's five sons.

The Hudson Family

———— ❧ ————

THE HUDSON FAMILY tree goes back seamlessly ten generations. A wealth of family information and documentation was gathered in the form of family descendant charts, photographs, and storied articles. The family's historical period begins as follows: "Henry Hudson was born 1500 and died 1555. He married Barbara. Child of Henry Hudson I and Barbara is: Henry Hudson II, b. 1541" (Ancestry.com 2017a). The following information about Henry Hudson III, who was born in 1570 in England, was a fascinating surprise to us. He was the famous explorer and navigator who discovered what became known as the Hudson River in New York (1609) while working for the Dutch East India Company, which hired him to find a northern route to Asia.

Yes, Robert Banks Cornelius Jr. is a direct descendant of Henry Hudson III, the famous explorer, and it all starts with the third generation of the Hudson family, when Richard Hudson I (1605–1657), the son of William Hudson II and his wife, Alice Turner, traveled from Staffordshire, England, to Northampton, Virginia, where he died in 1657. Richard Hudson I was known by the family as the "immigrant" Hudson. Richard Hudson I married Mary Hayes in 1638. She was a thirty-year-old widow and his second wife. When he married Mary, he gained at least two stepchildren and debt that was the value of the estate she inherited. Because his first wife's name is unknown, I question whether his son, Richard Hudson II, who was born in 1634 in Accomack, is the child of his first unknown wife or of Mary Bowman. Richard Hudson I is the fourth generation of the Hudson family. It is recorded that at age thirty, Richard Hudson I traveled from England on the ship *Safety* on August 10, 1635, from which he disembarked in Accomack County, Virginia, and eventually purchased and owned land on Hungars Creek, one of the oldest Eastern Shore settlements in the Virginia colony (Porter 2016).

In an e-mail message to Robert and me from Ancestry.com on April 1, 2014, we learned the following:

Richard Hudson was possibly a coastal trader, for he is mentioned as a mariner in 1642, captain of his own ship and his mate was Thomas Streete. His holdings of land, crops, a mill and warehouse, and livestock indicate his activities were likely local too.

He used the mark of the fleur-de-lis on his livestock, which was associated with Henry Alderman's coat of arms of the Hudson family. Richard Hudson, I did not like Maryland settlers, and it could have been because of the rivalry between Virginia and Maryland over Chesapeake trade. There were also religious differences, as most Marlyanders were Catholics. Richard Hudson I's two sons, Henry and Nicholas, were probably Quakers, and Nicholas's wife, Elizabeth Freeman, was a Maryland Quaker. Roy D. Hudson, another member of the Hudson family, wrote in his work that Richard Hudson I was a sailor who married a third time to Barbara Jacob, continued to live in Hungars Creek, and left a nuncupative (verbally witnessed) will in 1659, which took effect two years after his death.

We continued our research to find out more about this Hudson family of early British colonists who settled in Virginia 141 years before the American Revolution of 1776. In the "book entitled *Ye Kindome of Accawmacke or the Eastern Shore of Virginia in the Seventeenth Century* by Jennings Cropper Wise on page 137 between March 11, 1651 and the next 30 days, 116 signatures were collected from the people of Northampton County, Virginia, and Richard Hudson was among them" (Ancestry.com 2017). However, there is speculation that the signature could have belonged to Richard I or II, as the senior Richard Hudson did not die until 1657.

Richard Hudson II married Mary Bowman, the daughter of Robert Bowman, in 1658 in Accomack, Virginia. They were the parents of the following children: Richard Hudson III, born in 1660 in Henrico County,

Virginia; Robert Hudson, born in 1662 in Henrico County, Virginia; and William Hudson, born in 1668 in Henrico County, Virginia. Robert Banks Cornelius Jr. is a direct male descendant of Robert Hudson, as follows: Robert Hudson (1662–1750) married Mary Margaret Farquson (1663–1693) in Henrico County, Virginia. Their son is Henry Hudson IV (1700–1760), the sixth generation of the Hudson family.

Henry Hudson IV (1700–1760) and Mary Russell (1705–1806) had a son, Abraham Hudson (1729–1806; note that mother and son died the same year). Abraham Hudson married Elizabeth Tyler (1755–1827), and they were the parents of the eighth generation of the Hudson family, which consisted of twelve children. On Cherie Hudson's family tree on Ancestry.com, we found an extensively written newspaper article titled "Typical of Families Who Settled Area" that gave the following fascinating insight into the genealogy and familial histories of Abraham and Elizabeth (née Tyler) Hudson:

> When the former Cherokee Indian lands of Greenville County were opened to settlement in 1784, one of the families attracted to settle here was that of Abraham Hudson, who moved to a land grant dated July 12, 1784, and began developing a tract of 1,000 acres on Rocky Creek.

> The family was Episcopalian, tobacco planters from Bedford County, Va., from where hogsheads of tobacco were rolled to Lynchburg, the nearest market.

> Abraham Hudson had inherited a large estate because his father, an emigrant from England, had sympathy for him; he had an arm injury that was caused by a nurse letting him fall into a fire as an infant. The estate included then two plantations on the James River in Virginia.

> When Abraham Hudson brought his family to South Carolina it was with full support of his Maryland wife, Elizabeth Tyler Hudson, related to the Russells of Maryland and a cousin of President Tyler.

The president the article referred to was John Tyler, the tenth president of the United States (April 6, 1841 to March 3, 1845). After reading this news-paper article, we were stunned by the realization that Robert is related to Henry Hudson the explorer and also to President John Tyler through Abraham and Elizabeth Hudson's son, Burrell Vaudry Hudson (1769–1852), who lived to be eighty-four years old. He married Sarah W. Yeargin (1783–1860) in 1800 in Greenville, South Carolina, and they had ten children. Burrell and Sarah's second son and fifth child, Madison E. Hudson (1814–1866), was the first husband of Frances Henrietta Blackburn, who was the daughter of Lewis Blackburn and Polly Vann, citizens of the New Echota Cherokee nation capital who were removed from Calhoun, Georgia, in 1838 on the Trail of Tears to Oklahoma.

Madison E. and Frances Blackburn were legally married on January 2, 1840, in Forsyth, Georgia (Ancestry.com 1997). We now understand they must have met through the neighborly connection and between Lewis Blackburn and Alfred Hudson before and after they were moved on the Trail of Tears from Calhoun, Georgia, to Oklahoma. We also discovered they separated and divorced between 1844 and 1852, as Madison E. Hudson's name is not on either the Cherokee or Dawes Rolls. It is likely Frances and Madison lived together awhile before and after the birth of their son, Lewis, in Forsyth, Georgia. When the marriage ended in 1851, Frances chose to live with her parents in Oklahoma Indian Territory, where she and her son were safe and well accommodated.

It is imperative we elaborate more about Burrell Vaudry Hudson and how he became a fourth-generation paternal great-grandfather of Robert Banks Cornelius Jr. Burrell had a son, Henry B. Hudson (1816–1880), also known as Prince Hudson *outside* of his marriage to Sarah Washington Yeargin. Henry B. Hudson's mother is unknown, but he was born in Greenville, South Carolina. Like his father, Burrell, Henry B. Hudson was a slave owner (FamilySearch 2017b) while residing with his wife, Sarah Ellen (née Childers) Hudson (1826–?), in Wayneville, Houston, Georgia. At first, we were puzzled. Henry B. Hudson was a slave owner in Georgia, and he and his wife, Sarah, were recorded as free white citizens of the Muscogee Creek Indian Territory of Georgia in 1850. The Banks/Ashley family story was that Sarah was born on the Cherokee Reservation and was a full-blood Cherokee. Mind you, they did not know her maiden name or who her parents were, let alone the Cherokee Indian connection. It was during a telephone conversation with Robert's first cousin Elaine Collins that we learned she found, years ago, information about Burrell Vaudry Hudson, Henry B. Hudson, and Sarah Ellen (née Childers) Hudson, but we filled in the gaps by researching and discovering more documented information that helps complete the true story of the families' genealogy. We also had to face the true facts that the Blackburn and Hudson families were mixed-race white/Indian and that the families' financial, political, and geographical circumstances would dictate whether they would be considered white or Native American. We believe Henry B. Hudson's mother was Native American (Cherokee) and perhaps died in childbirth, which would explain why there is no record of her and that his father, Burrell, raised him.

BURRELL VAUDRY HUDSON PATERNAL FOURTH-GENERATION
GREAT-GRANDFATHER
TO ROBERT BANKS CORNELIUS JR.

Burrell Vaudry Hudson was a very handsome man. Based on a photo we found, you can tell by his clothing and gold-jeweled accessories that he was born into a wealthy family. He was a certified architect/builder, and his name was recorded as such pertaining to the building of the Hurricane Tavern in Spartanburg County, South Carolina, as noted in an e-mail we received on April 14, 2015, from New York City HC. The historic functions of the property/dwelling were domestic, commercial, and agricultural. It was also subcategorized as a single dwelling general store for processing and storage, with agricultural fields. You can read more about the details of Hurricane Tavern (a.k.a. Workman Farm) through the South Carolina Department of Archives and History website at http://www.nationalregis-ter.sc.gov/spartanburg/S10817742047/. The thirty buildings that make up the district are still standing, and you can buy a drink at the bar in the Hurricane Tavern.

On the 1840 federal census record, Burrell Vaudry Hudson and his family were listed as free white persons (six in number) with three slaves living in Greenville, South Carolina (Ancestry.com 2010a). Twenty years later, Burrell is recorded on the 1860 federal census record as living only with his wife, Sarah, and son, Ezkiel (Ancestry.com 2009b). Both men were listed as farmers in the Rocky Creek Division in the county of Greenville, South Carolina. Burrell lived in Greenville throughout his adult life despite being born in Virginia. His two sons, Madison E. Hudson and Henry B. Hudson, who were born in South Carolina, married and lived in different counties in Georgia during their adult lives, thus proving the Abraham Hudson family were wealthy landowners and slaveholders. Burrell Vaudry Hudson died in 1861 and in his will and testament dated April, 3 1852, he left his son Madison E. Hudson only one dollar, and Henry B. Hudson was not even mentioned. This led us to further speculate that Henry B. Hudson was half Native American and white and raised by his mother while being financially supported by his father, Burrell Vaudry Hudson.

USDI/NPS NRHP Registration Form   Page 3

Hurricane Tavern   Spartanburg County, South Carolina
Name of Property   County and State

---

8. Statement of Significance

Applicable National Register Criteria
(Mark "x" in one or more boxes for the criteria qualifying the property for National Register listing)
X A   Property is associated with events that have made a significant contribution to the broad patterns of our history.
__ B   Property is associated with the lives of persons significant in our past.
X C   Property embodies the distinctive characteristics of a type, period, or method of construction or represents the work of a master, or possesses high artistic values, or represents a significant and distinguishable entity whose components lack individual distinction.
__ D   Property has yielded, or is likely to yield information important in prehistory or history.

Criteria Considerations
(Mark "X" in all the boxes that apply.)
__ a   owned by a religious institution or used for religious purposes.
__ b   removed from its original location.
__ c   a birthplace or a grave.
__ d   a cemetery.
__ e   a reconstructed building, object, or structure.
__ f   a commemorative property.
__ g   less than 50 years of age or achieved significance within the past 50 years.

Areas of Significance   **Period of Significance**
(Enter categories from instructions)   ca. 1811-ca. 1950
  Architecture
  Agriculture
                                                   Significant Dates
                                                       ca. 1811
                                                       ca. 1850
                                                       ca. 1920

Significant Person   **Cultural Affiliation**
(Complete if Criterion B is marked above)

                                                   Architect/Builder
                                                     Workman, Clarence Hix
                                                     Hudson, Burrell V.
Narrative Statement of Significance
Explain the significance of the property on one or more continuation sheets.)

---

9. Major Bibliographical References

(Cite the books, articles, and other sources used in preparing this form on one or more continuation sheets.)

Previous documentation on file (NPS):   Primary location of additional data:
__ preliminary determination of individual listing (36 CFR 67) has been   X State Historic Preservation Office
   requested.   __ Other State agency
__ previously listed in the National Register   __ Federal agency
__ previously determined eligible by the National Register __ Local government
__ designated a National Historic Landmark   __ University
__ recorded by Historic American Buildings Survey # ____   __ Other
__ recorded by Historic American Engineering Record # ____ Name of repository:
                                                            S.C. Dept. of Archives and History

BURRELL V. HUDSON, ARCHITECT HURRICANE TAVERN,
SPARTANBURG, SOUTH CAROLINA - CIRCA 1811 TO 1860

Through our genealogy research on Burrell Vaudry Hudson and based on data supplied by Richard Bradley Hudson and the Hudson family tree compiled on March 6, 1928, we found that Patience Crain and Sarah Mahaffey were stated as his wives. Patience Crain was married to a man named Burrell Hudson, who at the conclusion of the American Revolution was one of several brothers who settled as farmers in the Carolinas and Georgia. One of the brothers was Burrell Hudson and he made Georgia his home, and here he met and married Miss Patience Crain. But soon afterward the "westward spirit" asserted itself and the young couple migrated to East Tennessee, where they picked a farm on Clinch River, some thirty miles north of where Knoxville was later built. And after a few years of frontier struggle here, they pushed further westward—across the mountains—and located on Calf River, near Sparta, White County, Tennessee.

Burrell Vaudry Hudson was seven years old when the American Revolutionary War began in 1776. He did not live in Tennessee for his entire life. Burrell Hudson died in 1819 in White County, Tennessee, and left a widow, Patience Crain, three daughters, and six sons who served in the American Revolutionary War. Thus, they were two different people with similar names. We could not find a marriage record for Sarah Mahaffey and Burrell Vaudry Hudson, and this is logical because Sarah Mahaffey was three years old as recorded on the 1850 census record of Greenville, South Carolina, and Burrell Vaudry Hudson was eighty-one years old at that time.

Henry B. Hudson (1816–1880) was born in South Carolina to Burrell Vaudry Hudson outside of Burrell's marriage. We are still researching genealogy information about Henry's mother and early childhood. He owned twenty-one slaves, and this information was discovered as stated on "Slave Schedule 2. Slave Inhabitants in Wayneville in the County of Houston State of Georgia, enumerated by me on the 1st day of October 1850 Asst. Marshall" (Ancestry.com 2010b). The slave schedule does not list the names of each slave, only their age, sex, and color.

Henry B. Hudson married Sarah Ellen Childers (1826–?) on January 1, 1845, in Houston County, Georgia (Ancestry.com 2013). The Huston-Ashley family tree states, "Sarah was born 1820 in Cherokee Nation, Ga., and died date unknown in Dry Branch, Twiggs County, Ga. She married B. Hudson (a.k.a. Prince)." Henry B. Hudson and Sarah Ellen (née Childers)

UNITED STATES CENSUE (SLAVE SCHEDULE), WAYNEVILLE,
HOUSTON COUNTY, GEORGIA - 1850

HOUSTON, MUSCOGEE, AND TALBOT COUNTIES, GEORGIA MARRIAGES, 1826-1852 HENRY B HUDSON AND SARAH CHILDERS MARRIAGE REGISTER

had a daughter, Nancy Hudson (1854–1922), who was born in Houston County, Georgia. On May 19, 2016, we visited Mrs. Willie G. Sampson in Dry Branch, Twiggs County, Georgia, and she verbally confirmed that Nancy Olivet Hudson was born in Houston County, Georgia, and died and was buried in Dry Branch, Twiggs County, Georgia. Nancy had an elder brother named Edward Hudson who was born in 1848, but there was no record of his death; perhaps he died young. There was another brother, Frank Hudson, who was born in 1835. He was not Sarah Hudson's son because she was not married to Henry B. Hudson in 1835 and certainly did not birth a child at the age of nine.

The US census of 1850 listed Henry B. Hudson and Sarah Hudson as "Free Inhabitants in Wayneville District in the County of Houston State of Georgia" (Ancestry.com 2009a). This meant they were free white people living in their own house. Henry B. Hudson was a farmer, and the value of the real estate he owned was $2,500. He also clearly stated he was born in

South Carolina. His wife, Sarah Hudson, noted her state of birth as Georgia. What we question on this 1850 census record is their stated ages: Henry is listed as twenty-six years old and Sarah as twenty-four. If Henry B. Hudson was born in 1826, it is not possible he could have had a son born in 1835, as it would mean he had a child at the age of nine. Henry B. Hudson's correct birth year is 1816, and it is more than likely he did have a son when he was nineteen years old in 1835. We were more than happy and surprised to see on the 1850 census record that Sarah Hudson's parents, John S. Childers and her stepmother, Mariah Childers, and her step-siblings lived only one house down from theirs. Sarah's father was a farmer, as was her step-brother George (age sixteen), and their real estate was valued at $1,500.

1850CENSUSIMAGES - HENRY B. & SARAH HUDSON
MUSCOGEE CREEK TERRITORY GEORGIA

On July 31, 1867, Henry B. Hudson signed what was known as the Ironclad Oath with the signature of "Prince Hudson, Col." (Ancestry.com 2012a). We don't believe that anyone in Robert Banks Cornelius Jr.'s family engaging in the family's genealogy research noticed the "Col." ending Prince Hudson's signature. Henry B. (Prince) Hudson was a slave owner who was recorded as "colored" (Col.) next to his signature on the registration card of qualified voters. We believe Henry B. Hudson was likely the child of a Native American mother, perhaps a Cherokee from South Carolina, and his father, Burrell Vaudry Hudson, who was white, was born, raised, and died in South Carolina. It is well known that Native Americans were referred to and recorded as colored by the white government authorities as a means of illegitimately confiscating property from the various Native American tribes in the southern states during the 1800s based on racial status and the enslavement of Native peoples.

All black and white men who had served in either the Union or Confederate Armies and returned to the eleven Southern states after the end of the Civil War (1865) were required to sign and swear their allegiance to the US government as citizens participating in the reconstruction of the ten Southern states. The swearing in and signing the Ironclad Oath permitted the men to vote in state and federal elections. Yes, black men were granted the right to vote and actually paid state poll taxes in the South and North to exercise their freedom and civil rights as enfranchised citizens of the United States of America. What became known as Radical Reconstruction under the Republican Congress from 1866 to 1877 blocked the cautious and moderate approaches to granting civil rights to freedmen. The freedmen were considered as follows:

The Cherokee, Choctaw and Creek nations were among those Native American tribes that held enslaved African Americans before and during the American Civil War. They supported the Confederacy during the war, supplying some warriors in the West, as they were promised their own state if the Confederacy won. After the end of the war, the US required these tribes to make peace treaties, and to emancipate their slaves.

They were required to offer full citizenship in their tribes to those Freedmen who wanted to stay with the tribes. Numerous families had intermarried by that time or had other personal ties. If freedmen left the tribes, they would become US citizens. (Wikipedia 2017)

We could not determine exactly which year Henry, Sarah, and their children moved from Wayneville, Houston County, Georgia, to Dry Branch, Twiggs County, Georgia. We researched the 1870 US census records and saw the names of B. Hudson and Sarah Hudson living in their home and one house down from their daughter, Nancy (née Hudson) Ashley, who lived in the home of the Thomas family (Ancestry.com 2009c). What is very interesting is that Henry, Sarah, and their daughter, Nancy, were recorded as black on the 1870 census record, yet Henry and Sarah Hudson were recorded as free white persons living in Wayneville, Houston County, Georgia, on the 1850 census record. According to the Georgia Census Record, Dry Branch, Twiggs County, Georgia, in 1880, Sarah Hudson's information was recorded as follows: "Age: 52, Race: Black, Date of Birth: around 1828, Occupation: Housekeeper and the widowed mother-in-law who was living in the household of Griffin and Nancy (née Hudson) Ashley and six of their 11 children." We were intrigued when we saw Sarah Ellen Hudson's name recorded on the 1883 Hester Roll (1884 Hester Roll and Index of Eastern Cherokee; see USGenWeb Census Project 2017).

It is more than likely she was visiting her nephew-in-law, Lewis Blackburn Hudson, and his family, who had been living in Cons Creek, Cherokee, Georgia, since 1870. We have not found any information as to where and when Sarah Ellen (née Childers) Hudson was buried and died. She was fifty-two in 1880, and she would have been fifty-five in 1883. During our visit to Dry Branch on May 19, 2012, we physically searched for Sarah Ellen Hudson's gravesite at the Old Marion Church but did not find it. This has remained a relevant mystery, and we should resolve the issue when we attend the Banks family homecoming on August 14, 2018, at Old Marion Church.

Hester Roll - 1883

CHEROKEE REMOVAL HESTER ROLL 1883

As mentioned earlier, Lewis Blackburn Hudson (1841–1923) was the grandson of Lewis Blackburn and Polly Blackburn and the only son of Madison E. Hudson and Frances Henrietta (née Blackburn) Hudson. He was also the grandson of Burrell Vaudry Hudson and the nephew of Henry B. (Prince) Hudson. He was born in Forsyth County, Georgia, on February 10, 1841, which was the same county his parents were married in. His early

119

life was spent in Coo-wee-scoo-wee, Cherokee Nation, Indian Territory, Oklahoma, where he lived with his mother and grandparents. On the 1870 US Federal Census, he was listed as a white male, age twenty-nine, living in Cons Creek, Cherokee, Georgia, with his wife, Nancy M. Hudson, son, Harrison A. Hudson, and daughter, Sarah F. Hudson. The 1880 census has the family living in the same residence with five more children, one female bearing the name of Frances Hudson, and one male bearing the name of Burrell Hudson. Lewis Blackburn Hudson and his wife, Nancy M. (Malinda) Hudson, probably met and married in Coo-wee-scoo-wee (which became known as Chelsea, Oklahoma). After realizing Lewis Blackburn Hudson returned to and lived in Georgia as an adult, we researched Georgia property tax digests from 1793 to 1892 (Ancestry. com 2011) and Georgia wills, probates, land, tax, and criminal records from 1889 to 2013 (Ancestry.com 2017b) and saw where he paid property taxes on land in Cherokee County, Georgia (1874–1877 and 1878–1881), Yellow Creek, Dawson, Georgia (1877–1887), and McConnell, Cherokee County, Georgia (1878–1881 and 1885–1887). His ownership of properties throughout Georgia bears witness to the wealth of the Blackburn and Hudson families that was handed down from one generation to the next.

In the US school catalogs from 1765 to 1935, Lewis Blackburn Hudson's name appears as residing in Milton, Wisconsin, in 1854 (Ancestry.com 2012b). He was thirteen years old and perhaps was living in the town of Milton with his parents or other relatives. Joseph Goodrich founded the town of Milton in 1844 and also established Milton Academy (City of Milton 2017), which is where we believe Lewis Blackburn Hudson received his early education. At the age of twenty-one (1862), Lewis served in the Confederate army in Cobb's Legion State of Georgia (FamilySearch 2017a). On August 22, 1867, Lewis Blackburn Hudson swore his allegiance (Ironclad Oath) to the US federal government and signed the *Georgia, Return of Qualified Voters and Reconstruction Oath Books* at his residence in Cherokee County, Georgia.

Those of you who have Native American ancestry have probably referred to the Dawes Roll of 1898 to 1907 to research family members of the Five Civilized Tribes—Cherokee, Chickasaw, Choctaw, Creek, and Seminole— who were forcibly moved and relocated by the US government's military troops between 1836 and 1839 from the states of Georgia, Tennessee, North and South Carolina, Florida, Alabama, and Mississippi to what became known as Indian Territory in Oklahoma. President Andrew Johnson signed the Indian Removal Act in 1830. The US congressional plan to remove the five civilized tribal nations deliberately made Native American lands in these previously mentioned states available for white Americans and European immigrants to settle on. The Dawes Act of February 8, 1887, was signed into law as a means of determining the citizens of the Native American tribes that were moved. The Dawes Commission prepared the new citizenship rolls for each tribe. Those who survived the Trail of Tears, such as white, Native, and/or black peoples, had to apply for the citizenship of their respective tribes, and it was the Dawes Commission that approved each application. Once approved, the applicant's name was placed on the respective tribal roll, and an allotted share of communal land was approved for individual tribe members.

Robert Banks Cornelius Jr.'s ancestor Lewis Blackburn Hudson and his family's names were found on the Dawes Roll of 1898 (Roll No. 13093) as residing in Chelsea, Oklahoma. We even found the names of Lewis Blackburn (the white grandfather of Lewis Blackburn Hudson) and Polly (née Vann) Blackburn (the full-blood Cherokee grandmother of Lewis Blackburn Hudson). We chose to do more complete research and discovered copies of the original documents. First was the standard written application completed by each applicant "for such share as may be due me of the funds appropriated by the Act of Congress approved June 30, 1906, in accordance with the decrees of the Court of Claims of May 18, 1905, and May 28, 1906, in favor of the Eastern Cherokees. The evidence of identity is herewith subjoined." Lewis Blackburn Hudson completed his application on October 8, 1906. Second, Lewis Blackburn Hudson had also applied for daughter Amanda Hudson to be placed on the Cherokee Rolls through testimony he had given before the Department of the Interior, Commission to the Five Civilized Tribes, Chelsea, I. T., on November 16, 1900. Lewis Blackburn Hudson stated in his testimony that he wanted his wife, Nancy Malinda (née Williams) Hudson (also known as Nannie), to be considered for Cherokee citizenship. His daughter, Amanda Hudson, was "duly listed for enrollment as Cherokee citizens by blood." But his wife, Nannie, a white person, was refused because her name did not appear on any Cherokee Nation roll or in the certificate of admission that Lewis Blackburn Hudson had presented before the Commission of the Five Civilized Tribes. On the thirteenth US census, Lewis, Nannie, and Amanda Hudson were living in Township 1, Rogers, Oklahoma, and their race was shown as Indian (Native American) despite the fact that Lewis's father and paternal grandfather were white. Nonetheless, he was granted land by the Dawes Commission to settle on because he had proven his maternal grandmother, Polly (née Vann) Blackburn, was a full-blood Cherokee Indian.

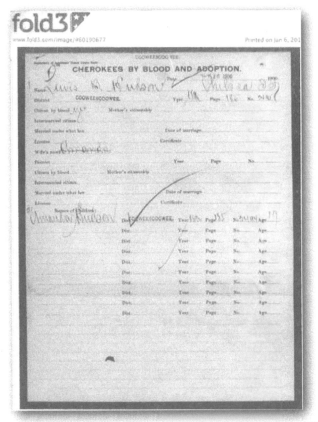

LEWIS BLACKBURN HUDSON'S CHEROKEE BY BLOOD AND
ADOPTION APPLICATION FOR DAUGHTER AMANDA HUDSON
- DAWES COMMISSION - CHELSEA, OKLAHOMA 1900

The Childers, Chapman, and Fuqua Families

—————— ⁊ ——————

JOHN S. (SPANN) Childers was born on February 24, 1799. He was the father of Sarah Ellen (née Childers) Hudson and the grandfather of Nancy Olivet (née Hudson) Ashley. John S. Childers's first wife was Permelia Burton (1800–1829), and they were married in Elbert County, Georgia, on January 4, 1821, where they resided for nearly ten years. John and Permelia had two daughters, Martha Ann and Sarah Ellen Childers. It was one year after the birth of their second daughter, Sarah Ellen, that Permelia Childers died in 1829.

Sarah Ellen Hudson (Hudson 1805 – 2005)

Photo Gallery: FamilySearch Memories

Born about 1820 – 1828 in Georgia, Cherokee Nation: Spouse: B Hudson (aka Prince)

SARAH ELLEN HUDSON (NEE CHILDERS), SECOND-GENERATION GREAT-GRANDMOTHER OF ROBERT BANKS CORNELIUS JR – STEPHENS' FAMILY PUBLIC TREE ANCESTRY.COM - SEPTEMBER 2016

John S. (Spann) Childers married Mariah Chapman in 1833. John and Mariah had five children and resided in Wayneville, Houston County, Georgia, in 1850. According to a blog post, John S. Childers and two of his sons with Mariah "resided at the Childers Mansion at Pleasant Hill, Louisiana where the {American Civil War} Battle of Pleasant Hill took place April 5, 1864." Before this period in American history, John S. Childers's daughter Sara (Sarah) was mentioned in a book titled *History of Gwinnett County, Georgia: 1818–1943, Vol. 1* (Flanigan 1943), along with the names of other prominent young and eligible women for marriage who were living in that county in the 1840s. In 1850, John S. Childers was living with his wife, Mariah, and five of his six children in Hayneville, Houston County, Georgia. They were living next door to his son-in-law Henry B. Hudson and his daughter Sarah Ellen. The two men were slaveholding farmers who moved out of Houston County, Georgia, before the start of the American Civil War in 1861.

John S. Childers died on June 9, 1859, and was buried in Old Pleasant Hill Cemetery, De Soto Parish, Louisiana. John and Mariah's second daughter, Julia, married W. D. Gooch, the son of another prominent family in Pleasant Hill. The genealogical records of the elite white families throughout the United States were kept up to date to secure inheritances of land and money. The names Childers and Childress were and still are interchangeable, and they are related no matter which way one spells this surname. It was no surprise when we discovered that Thomas Childress's family was from Henrico County, Virginia (like the Hudson family), and that they moved to South Carolina and to Walton County, Georgia. Most of these white families intermarried with the Cherokee and Creek Indians of the Carolinas and Georgia, and throughout the years mixed with generations of free peoples of color and enslaved blacks.

Mariah (née Chapman) Childers (1808–1885) was born in Georgia and married John S. Childers in 1833. Mariah's parents were Ambrose Chapman (1785–1866) and Elizabeth Stone (the dates of her birth and death are unknown). She had four siblings. Her parents were married on January 13, 1806, and her mother, Elizabeth, gave birth in the years 1806,

1807, 1808, 1810, and 1811. We noticed her father married a second wife, Elizabeth Andrews, on May 27, 1813, and one son was born during this marriage. When Ambrose Chapman turned sixty-eight, he married his third wife, Martha Ann Seymour, and she bore two children during the marriage. As stated in a written in-memoriam tribute, Ambrose Chapman "was for thirty-five years a professor of religion, and a member of the Baptist Church." He was a native of Chatham County, North Carolina, and resided in one of the cities for at least twenty years before moving to Warren County, Georgia, where he met and married his first wife, Elizabeth Stone, at age twenty-one.

Ambrose Chapman's parents were John Chapman (born between 1750 and 1760 in Chatham County, North Carolina, and died in 1798 in Warren County, Georgia), and Mildred Fuqua (1755–1830). Mildred was born in Halifax County, North Carolina, and her earliest ancestor, William Fuqua I (1769–1838), was from Amelia County, Virginia. This particular genealogy line of the Fuqua family "almost assuredly descends from Guillaume Fouquet (alias Gill Fuquett/Gille Fugett/Gill Fucque/Gil Fucket/others) who married Jane Eyre (Ayre) in Hinrico County, VA, in 1687. Guillaume was a French Huguenot who came to the Charles City, VA, area well before the main Huguenot migration to America." Mildred Fuqua was the paternal grandmother of Mariah (née Chapman) Childers, the step great-grandmother of Sarah Ellen (née Childers) Hudson and the step great-great-grandmother of Nancy Olivet Hudson, who was Robert Banks Cornelius Jr.'s paternal great-grandmother. As you can see, again there is a genealogical connection to Henrico County, Virginia, in the 1600s, just as there was for the Hudson family.

From this point on you will read about Robert Banks Cornelius Jr.'s genealogical connections with the Ashley, Banks, Hudson, Cornelius, Solomon, Thomas, Houston, and Glover families. Some of their ancestors were born in Dry Branch, Twiggs County, Georgia as early as 1815, and most of their descendants became landowners, businessmen and women, and educators during the Reconstruction Era of 1867-1877.

A Brief History of Twiggs County, Georgia

Twiggs County was established through a proposed bill in the Georgia State Legislature on November 14, 1809. The new county was separated from Wilkinson County and named in honor of Major General John Twiggs a famous American Revolutionary soldier from Georgia. On December 14, 1809 the bill was passed and became law.

Marion was the first county seat and is geographically located in the center of the State of Georgia. The geologists who were sent from the State Department of Natural Resources and the United States Geologic Survey located the State of Georgia center in a swamp area where the two creeks Turvin and Savage Creek intersect. A bronze marker was erected to identify the location. We now know and appreciate the history of the historic marker that was placed in front of Old Marion Baptist Church, the exact church Robert's familial descendants built in 1883. The marker is approximately 1.1 miles from the bronze marker the geologists placed as the 'heart' of Georgia. I and Robert Banks Cornelius Jr. travelled from New York City to Dry Branch, Twiggs County, Georgia five times to visit his family members and attend church service where the marker stands in front of Old Marion Baptist Church, at the intersection of Bullard and Marion Ripley Road

The Ephraim Faulk Ashley Family

———— ৡ ————

EPHRAIM FAULK ASHLEY (born in 1815 or 1816 and died in 1890) was born in Twiggs County, Georgia. At age eighteen, Ephraim's first son, Nick Ashley (1834–1909), was born in Twiggs County, Georgia. Nick was also known as Lord Nelson Peck. The family story is that Nick Ashley got into very serious trouble with a white man and had to run away from Georgia before the authorities arrested him. Nick ran to the state of Ohio and never returned to Georgia. Ephraim Ashley had a second son, Griffin Ashley (1844–1923), who also was born in Twiggs County, Georgia, and met and married Nancy Olivet Hudson. On the 1870 census record for Twiggs County, Nancy and Griffin are living together with their daughter, Zilpha, two sons, Seaborn and Nick, and another child named Andrew Young. They lived next door to Nancy's parents, B. Hudson and Sarah Hudson. We strongly believe Ephraim's first two sons, Nick and Griffin, were born to two different mothers, and we could not trace Ephraim's parents. Ephraim Faulk Ashley's wife, Lucinda Grady, was a full-blood Creek Indian, and he was twenty-seven years older than his wife. On the 1870 census record for Twiggs County, Georgia, Ephraim and Lucinda were listed as mulatto and living with their five children: Efrom, Ann, Alfred, Dellar, and Cisero Ashley.

When we could not find Ephraim Ashley or his first two sons on the 1860 census record for Twiggs County, Georgia, the next step was to search the last names of slave owners in Twiggs County before and up to 1865. We speculate that William Faulk (born in 1805 in Marion, Twiggs County, Georgia) was the slave owner of Ephraim Faulk Ashley and more than likely inherited Ephraim, because he was not old enough to be Ephraim's father. William Faulk is listed as a slave owner on the 1850 and 1860 US census slave schedules (Ancestry.com 1999; FamilySearch

2017b). Another interesting fact we found about William Faulk is that he applied for and was granted a presidential pardon on August 4, 1865, from participating as a Confederate soldier in the Civil War "because he had 'commercial' property worth $20,000" (Ancestry.com 2008).

According to the United States Civil War and Later Pension Index, 1861–1917, Ephraim Faulk Ashley was recorded as a black Civil War soldier who served in the "Colored Light Artillery; Military Company: B; Military Regiment: 2" (FamilySearch 2016). He fought in the Union army in one or more of the nine batteries (A–I in Tennessee, Virginia, Mississippi, Arkansas, and South Carolina) of the Second Regiment, United States Colored Light Artillery. We plan to travel to the African American Civil War Memorial in Washington, DC, to search for Ephraim Ashley's name (listed by military unit) among "the over two hundred thousand names listed on metal plates along the front and sides of long, curved walls forming a semi-circle around the central statute" (Hatlie 2006).

EPHRAIM ASHLEY UNITED STATES CIVIL WAR AND
LATER PENSION INDEX, 1861 TO 1917

Ephraim Faulk Ashley's second son, Griffin Ashley (1844–1923), and his wife, Nancy Olivet (née Hudson) Ashley (1854–1922), had ten children, all of whom were born in Twiggs County, Georgia: Nick Ashley, Lula (Tish) Ashley, Sylvia (Silvie) Ashley, Seaborn Ashley, Emma Ashley, Edward Drayton Ashley, Minnie Ashley, Fred Lee Ashley, Alberta Ashley, and Olivet (Ollie) Ashley.

Grandma Nancy Hudson Ashley

GRANDMA NANCY OLIVET HUDSON (NEE ASHLEY)
DAUGHTER OF HENRY B. HUDSON (A.K.A. PRINCE) AND
SARAH ELLEN HUDSON (NEE CHILDERS)

Their daughter Alberta (Aunt Bird) Ashley was born on February 18, 1891, and she married John Banks Jr., who was born in Twiggs County, Georgia, on March 3, 1889. Alberta and John were the paternal grandparents of Robert Banks Cornelius Jr. Alberta and John Banks Jr. married on December 28, 1910. A family member brought to our attention that Griffin Ashley was recorded as deceased in 1880. We immediately questioned this because his and Nancy's daughter, Alberta Ashley, was born in 1891, a year before their last child, Olivet (Ollie) Ashley. We could not find a record of Griffin Ashley's death in 1880, but he was recorded on the 1880 US census as living with his wife, Nancy, and three sons and three daughters. We also found his name in the Georgia property tax digests for 1880 (Ancestry.com 2011). This information more than proves Griffin Ashley was alive and voting as a black man in Twiggs County, Georgia, in 1880 because the enfranchised black men (meaning those who were registered to vote) had to pay a poll tax before they could vote in general and local elections in the eleven southern states.

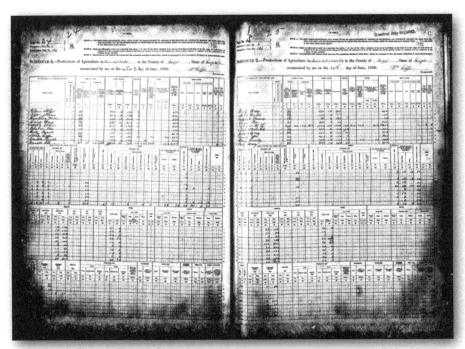

GRIFFIN ASHLEY - GEORGIA AGRICULTURE LAND
RECORDS 1880 TWIGGS COUNTY, GEORGIA

In an interview on May 9, 2016, Mrs. Willie Stephens informed us that three Ashley sisters married three brothers from the Cornelius family. Alberta's mother, Nancy Olivet Ashley, was a trained midwife and worked in the Dry Branch and Jeffersonville, Twiggs County, communities for many years. The following families lived in the Twiggs County community and are related to the Ashley and Banks families through marriage: Solomon, Thomas, Stephens, Cornelius, Shinholster, Baisley, Glover, Wimberly, Green, and Peck.

The Harry Banks Family

─────── ❦ ───────

THE BANKS FAMILY tree begins with Harry Banks (1816–?). The Banks family was from south Macon, Georgia, but we could not find any written information as to how Harry Banks came to Twiggs County, Georgia. Mrs. Elaine (née Banks) Collins, the first cousin of Robert Banks Cornelius, Jr., verbally confirmed to me through one of many telephone conversations about the family that the Banks are of Creek Indian heritage, and more precisely, they are Muscogee Creek Indians from southeastern Georgia. When we searched the Twiggs County, Georgia, 1860 slave census schedules and the 1870 census surname matches for African Americans, we were surprised the surnames of Hudson and Banks were not found as slaveholders in Twiggs County during those years (Ancestry.com 2002). In the Georgia property tax digests for 1793 to 1892, Harry Banks's name does appear, along with Ephraim Ashley, Harry Banks Jr., Ephraim Glover, Zack Stephens, Dick Thomas, and Henry Stephens, as each paying a one-dollar poll tax, and they are included on the freedmen lists as employees of former Twiggs County slaveholders William L. Solomon, James T. Glover, and William Faulk (Ancestry.com 2011). After searching for more information, we found that a John Banks of Muscogee County, Georgia, was listed as the owner of twenty-three slaves in 1850, and his real estate value was $29,550. We speculated he might have been Harry Banks's former slave owner, meaning perhaps he sold Harry Banks to a slave owner in Twiggs County between 1850 and 1860.

We called Mrs. Elaine Collins with our findings, and she explained that Harry Banks had a connection with the Coombs Plantation in Virginia, but she had reached a brick wall regarding this part of the Banks family genealogy. We asked her about Edward Banks (1864–?) who was born in Virginia and went to New York State, becoming a well-to-do man who owned property in East Hampton, Long Island, New York. He married a Montauk Native American woman named Mariah Pharoah Johnson (1848–1936). Edward and Mariah Banks had one son, Junious Banks (1896-1964). Edward Banks had a daughter, Edith J. Banks, in 1882 who died at birth. Mrs. Collins did not give us any new information pertaining to Edward and Mariah Banks. We did not find the missing link pertaining to the Harry Banks and Edward Banks familial connection, but there must be something to this oral history because several Banks family members who live in Twiggs County, Georgia, have heard the story about their "rich" family member Edward Banks from Virginia who lived in New York.

The Twiggs County, Georgia, 1870 census record shows Harry Banks, a farm laborer, and his wife, Lucretia (née Solomon) Banks, living next door to W. L. Solomon, a white farmer. W. L. Solomon's real estate value was $5,000, and his personal estate value was $3,500. Harry and Lucretia were not property owners and did not have any personal items of value. It is obvious Harry Banks was a farm laborer on the Solomon farm, and he and Lucretia were recorded as black. On July 3, 2017, Mrs. Elaine Collins, Robert Banks Cornelius Jr.'s first cousin, called me and imparted more oral history about the Banks family: Lucretia (née Solomon) Banks (also known as Cressy) was the daughter of Ann Solomon. Ann Solomon, a half Cherokee Indian, became pregnant and had a quasi- marriage to a slave. Her grandfather was white and a relative of the Solomon plantation owners in Twiggs County, Georgia.

Harry and Lucretia Banks had eleven children: Lemuel Banks, Harry Banks, Emma Banks, Louisa Banks, Peggy Banks, John Banks, Lucinda Banks, Jeff Banks, Ann Banks, Indiana Banks, and Georgia Banks. Harry and Lucretia and their children, his mother-in-law, Ann Solomon (fifty-nine years old), and a male toddler named A. Jackson were recorded on the 1880 US census as living in Marion, Twiggs County, Georgia. Harry's occupation is listed as farmer, which meant he was now a land-owner. Harry Banks signed the *Georgia, Returns of Qualified Voters and Reconstruction Oath Books*, 1867–1869, on July 31, 1867, as a resident of

HARRY BANKS AND LUCRETIA BANKS (NEE SOLOMON) - SHARED ON MRS.
ELAINE COLLINS' PUBLIC FAMILY TREE - ANCESTRY.COM - JUNE 2017

Twiggs County, Georgia (Ancestry.com 2012). In 1910, Harry Banks Sr. was sixty-seven years old and living with his wife, Lucretia, and his grandsons Garfield Cabiness (age twenty) and Grand Curtis (age twenty-two) in Marion, Twiggs County, Georgia.

Jeff Banks (1870–1940) was the fourth son of Harry and Lucretia Banks and the father of John Banks Jr. His wife was Elaine Baisley (1870–?), who was also known as Lanie (or Laney) Banks. They had the following children: John Banks, Mary Lizzie Banks, Essie Banks, and Eva Banks. A Jeffrey Banks was listed on the 1870 US census as living with his maternal grandmother, Ann Solomon, and his older and younger siblings in the household of a couple named Ander and Rachel Prow, District 355, Twiggs County, Georgia. We wondered why Harry and Lucretia's children were in the household of Ander and Rachel Prow. Upon taking a closer look

HARRY BANKS - GEORGIA RETURNS QUALIFIED VOTERS & RECONSTRUCTION
OATH BOOKS 1867-1869

at one of the many Banks family trees, we noticed Jeffrey Banks (born in 1863) was a senior brother to Jeff Banks (born in 1870), and more than likely, Mr. and Mrs. Prow had taken in the Banks children after their mother, Lucretia Banks, had given birth to Jeff Banks. Jeff Banks's occupation was listed as farmer on his death certificate, which is dated December 4, 1940. He had been living in Jeffersonville, Georgia, and died of pneumonia. Interestingly, a young woman, Mary L. Hill, was the signee on his death certificate. Mary L. Hill is shown on a Banks family tree as a child of Jeff

Banks, but on the 1930 US census, in the household of Jefferson Banks and Lanie Banks, Mary L. Hill (age twenty-four) and Johnnie Hill (age thirty-one) are shown living with them. There is some confusion regarding the names because Jeff and Jefferson are two different brothers, and it was Jeff Banks who was married to Elaine (née Baisley) Banks.

John Banks Jr. was Alberta Ashley's first husband, and he died on June 4, 1918, in Twiggs County, Georgia, at the age of twenty-nine. He was a successful black businessman who owned land, a lumberyard, a store, and an automobile. He was a prominent and rising star in the Twiggs County community who contributed spiritually and financially to the community's well-known Old Marion Church. The church was organized on December 15, 1866, and is a national landmark located in the center of the state of Georgia. By 1871, Reverend A. Durham was its pastor, and Brother W. Pate was

MARRIAGE LICENSE - JOHN BANKS JR AND ALBERTA ASHLEY, PATERNAL GRAND PARENTS OF ROBERT BANKS CORNELIUS JR. - 1900 STATE OF GEORGIA TWIGGS COUNTY its secretary. Edward Drayton Ashley, the son of Griffin and Nancy Ashley, owned the land and donated it for the church site. In 1883, the church was rebuilt, and Reverend Sauley Cornelius was its pastor, along with the two deacons, Henry Stephens and Griffin Ashley, respectively. John Banks Jr. was named after his uncle. John's parents were Jeff Banks (1869–1940) and Elaine (née Baisley) Banks. Alberta (née Ashley) Banks (Aunt Bird) was the mother of five children—Robert Banks Sr., Lillian Banks, Chadwick Banks, Birdie Mae Banks, and John Quincy Banks—at the time her husband, John Banks Jr., was murdered. Some white community members approached him about selling his land, but when John Banks Jr. refused to sell, he was killed out of jealousy.

Zachary Cornelius (1874–1955) was Alberta (née Ashley) Banks's second husband, and they married in 1920. They had five children: Avarilla Cornelius, Lewis Henry Cornelius, Christine Cornelius, Nancy Mae Cornelius, and Zack Cornelius Jr. In an interview on May 9, 2016, Mrs. Willie G. Stephens informed us that three Ashley sisters married three brothers from the Cornelius family. Alberta's mother, Nancy Olivet Ashley, was a trained midwife and worked in the Dry Branch and Jeffersonville, Twiggs County, communities for many years. According to the 1900 US census record, Zachary Cornelius, age twenty-five, was living with his parents, Tim and Laura Cornelius, and five siblings in Bluff, Twiggs County, Georgia. On the 1940 US census record, Zachary Cornelius was listed as educated through the sixth grade and recorded as a farmer, age sixty-six, who rented the house he was living in with his wife, Alberta Cornelius, and their children and grandchildren. When Zachary and Alberta married, he became the stepfather to her five children. Robert Banks Sr. was Alberta and John Banks's eldest child, and as an adult, he would take on his stepfather's last name of Cornelius. Zachary Cornelius died on January 7, 1955, at the age of eighty, in Twiggs County, Georgia (Ancestry.com. 2001).

Robert Banks Cornelius Sr. (1911–1990) was born on November 14, 1911, in Twiggs County, Georgia. On the 1930 US census, he was recorded as eighteen years old, single, and son to his stepfather, Zachary Cornelius. In 1932 at age twenty, Robert (Banks) Cornelius married Louella Albritton

ZACHARIAH CORNELIUS GRAVESITE OLD MARION
CHURCH DRY BRANCH TWIGGS GEORGIA

ALBERTA CORNELIUS GRAVESITE OLD MARION
CHURCH DRY BRANCH TWIGGS GEORGIA

on May 17 in Twiggs County, Georgia. Robert and Louella had one son, John Banks Cornelius (1933–1996). Robert Banks Cornelius Sr. got into some serious trouble with his first wife's parents and had to leave Twiggs County. He moved to Atlanta, Georgia, and at first lived with his sisters. At the age of twenty-eight, he met Gladys Nash (born in 1917) in Atlanta, and they had six children: Robert Banks Cornelius Jr. (the author of this book), Virginia Banks Cornelius, Rayfield Banks Cornelius, Linda Banks Cornelius, Elaine Banks Cornelius, Wanda Banks Cornelius, and Brenda Banks Cornelius. There was also a stepdaughter, Gladys Williams. Robert Banks Cornelius Sr. was a foreman butcher at a company called White Division in Atlanta. He worked there for about forty years and retired when the company moved to the Midwest. Robert Banks Cornelius Sr. died on May 4, 1990 and was buried in Atlanta. On Saturday, June 3, 2017, Mrs. Gladys (née Nash) Banks Cornelius, Robert Banks Cornelius Jr.'s mother, celebrated her one hundredth birthday with family and friends in Atlanta. You can read more about her wonderful life in the book *We the Resilient: Wisdom for America from Women Born before Suffrage* (Benor and Fields-Meyer 2017).

Margie Shinholster who is my cousin was born and raised in Dry Branch, Twiggs County, Georgia. I and Professor Morehand-Olufade went to her home in Camden, New Jersey, in September 2012 to find out more genealogical information about our mutual families' past and present history. She told us to make sure we attended the "Homecoming" day celebration at the families' Old Marion Church, in Dry Branch, Twiggs County, Georgia on the second Sunday in August 2016 to greet and meet family members whom I was not familiar with but could answer my questions about the history of the following: the Ashley Plantation, the township of Jeffersonville, the founding of Old Marion Church, and property ownership of the Banks, Ashley, Thomas, Dinnards, Stephens, Whiteheads, Nixon, Reagan (or Riggins), Hudson, Rogers, Blackburn, Cosby, Houston, Horne, and Turner families. Margie told us everybody owned land, and it dates back before the Civil War, such as antebellum Georgia. The old graveyard is on Old Marion Road, and the house of my grandmother,

Alberta Banks (née Ashley) was by the church. Nancy Olivet Ashley's (née Hudson) ten children, every one of them had a house and ten acres around it. She confirmed the facts that the Banks family is connected with the Cherokee of New Echota Cherokee Capital, Calhoun, Georgia, and the Washitaw Nation of Monroe, Louisiana, and Edward Banks of Long Island, New York, and the Cornelius family is connected with the Choctaw of Alabama.

INSIDE OLD MARION BAPTIST CHURCH, DRY BRANCH,
TWIGGS COUNTY, GEORGIA - AUGUST 2017

What peaked Professor Morehand-Olufade's interest even further was during a face-to-face conversation I had with my cousin Margie at her home in Camden, New Jersey, in September 2017, we were discussing my trip in 2007 to visit our cousin Angela in Enid, Oklahoma. I told Margie it was while I was pumping gas into a van at a station in Tulsa, Oklahoma, that a gentleman walked up to me and asked if I was a member of the Banks family. I told him no, my name was Robert Cornelius Jr., and I knew nothing about the Banks family. He told me I had a very strong resemblance to the Banks family who are Creek Indians that live in Okmulgee County, Oklahoma.

Now remember, in 2007 I had no knowledge of my paternal family's genealogical history, and my father had run away from Dry Branch, Twiggs County, Georgia, because he got into some trouble with the law. When he got to Atlanta, Georgia, he chose to drop the last name of his biological father, John Banks, and go by the last name of his stepfather, Zachariah Cornelius. Margie shouted, "Oh my God!" She said the Ocmulgee River (of Macon, Georgia) ran behind our grandmother Alberta's house in Dry Branch, Twiggs County, Georgia, and she played and watched the adults fish in the river as a youngster along with her siblings and cousins. The genealogical research we have completed on the Banks family ties in very well with my Muscogee Creek (twenty thousand) ancestors who walked along the Trail of Tears and settled in Okmulgee County, Oklahoma, between 1836 and 1837. The history of the Muscogee (Creek) Nation is little known,

"as their people are descendants of a remarkable culture that, before 1500 AD, spanned all the region known today as the Southeastern United States. Early ancestors of the Muscogee constructed magnificent earthen pyramids along the rivers of this region as part of their elaborate ceremonial complexes. The historic Muscogee later built expansive towns within these same broad river valleys in the present states of Alabama, Georgia, Florida and South Carolina. The Muscogee were not one tribe but a union of several. This union evolved into a confederacy that, in the Euro-American described "historical period," was the most sophisticated political organization north of Mexico. Member tribes were called tribal towns. Within this political structure, each tribal town maintained political autonomy and distinct land holdings."

I did good research on my father's family, and it is all true. It makes me feel extremely good because I found documented information that confirms there are no myths about the paternal side of my family. This has been a long and fantastic journey. It took nearly eight years to find all the information, and it was well worth the trip. Thanks to the Creator for allowing me to successfully finish my autobiography. I no longer ask the question, Who am I? I now know who I am and very proud of it!

PROFESSOR DARNELL A. MOREHAND-OLUFADE (RIGHT)
AND ROBERT BANKS CORNELIUS, JR. (LEFT)
STANDING NEAR SCHOMBURG CENTER FOR RESEARCH IN BLACK CULTURE, HARLEM,
NEW YORK, FEBRUARY 1, 2018
PHOTO TAKEN BY: MS. TESS REESE

References

Ancestry.com. 1997. *Georgia, Compiled Marriages, 1754–1850* [database online]. Provo, UT: Ancestry.com Operations.

———. 1999. *Georgia, Compiled Census and Census Substitutes Index, 1790–1890* [database online]. Provo, UT: Ancestry.com Operations.

———. 2001. *Georgia, Death Index, 1919–1998* [database online]. Provo, UT: Ancestry.com Operations.

———. 2002. "Twiggs County, Georgia: Largest Slaveholders from 1860 Slave Census Schedules and Surname Matches for African Americans on 1870 Census." Accessed December 15, 2017. http://freepages.genealogy.rootsweb.ancestry.com/ ~ajac/gatwiggs.htm.

———. 2004. *Georgia Marriages, 1699–1944* [database online]. Provo, UT: Ancestry.com Operations.

———. 2008. *Confederate Applications for Presidential Pardons, 1865–1867* [database online]. Provo, UT: Ancestry.com Operations.

———. 2009a. *1850 United States Federal Census* [database online]. Provo, UT: Ancestry.com Operations.

———. 2009b. *1860 United States Federal Census* [database online]. Provo, UT: Ancestry.com Operations.

———. 2009c. *1870 United States Federal Census* [database online]. Provo, UT: Ancestry.com Operations.

———. 2010a. *1840 United States Federal Census* [database online]. Provo, UT: Ancestry.com Operations.

————. 2010b. *1860 US Federal Census—Slave Schedules* [database online]. Provo, UT: Ancestry.com Operations.

————. 2011. *Georgia, Property Tax Digests, 1793–1892* [database online]. Provo, UT: Ancestry.com Operations.

————. 2012a. *Georgia, Returns of Qualified Voters and Reconstruction Oath Books, 1867–1869* [database online]. Provo, UT: Ancestry.com Operations.

————. 2012b. *US, School Catalogs, 1765–1935* [database online]. Provo, UT: Ancestry.com Operations.

————. 2013. *Georgia, Marriage Records from Select Counties, 1828–1978* [database online]. Provo, UT: Ancestry.com Operations.

————. 2017a. "Descendants of Henry Hudson." Accessed December 14, 2017. http:// freepages.genealogy.rootsweb.ancestry.com/~jentaylor/DescendantsHenryHudson.htm.

————. 2017b. "Georgia Wills, Probates, Land, Tax, and Criminal." Accessed December 14. https://search.ancestry.com/Places/US/Georgia/Default.aspx?category=36.

Banks Cornelius, Jr., Robert. 'I Had a Dream' Poem: Published by Community Impact, Columbia University, TASC Speaks Summer 2014, page 8.

Benor, Sarah Bunin, and Tom Fields-Meyer. Eds. 2017. *We the Resilient: Wisdom from Women Born before Suffrage.* Eugene, OR: Luminare Press.

City of Milton. 2017. "History of Milton." Accessed December 14, 2017. http://www.ci.milton.wi.us/index.aspx?nid=114.

FamilySearch. 2016. "United States Civil War and Later Pension Index, 1861–1917." https://beta.familysearch.org/search/collection/1471019.

———. 2017a. "Georgia Civil War Service Records of Confederate Soldiers." https://training.familysearch.org/wiki/en/Georgia_Civil_War_Service_Records_of_Confederate_Soldiers_(FamilySearch_Historical_Records).

———. 2017b. "United States Census (Slave Schedule), 1850." Accessed December 14, 2017. https://www.familysearch.org/search/collection/1420440.

Flanigan, James C. 1943. *History of Gwinnett County, Georgia: 1818–1943, Vol. I.* Hapeville, GA: Tyler.

Hatlie, Mark. 2006. "African American Civil War Memorial, Washington, DC." June 19. http://www.sites-of-memory.de/main/DCafricanamericancivilwar.html.

Porter, Ronda Chesser. 2016. "Hudson Genealogy from Rudolph to Richard IV." The Domestic Curator, December 24. http://www.thedomesticcurator.com/2013/12/hudson-genealogy-from-rudolph-to.html.

Shadburn, Don, L. 1989. *Cherokee Planters in Georgia, 1832–1838: Historical Essays on Eleven Counties in the Cherokee Nation of Georgia.* Roswell, GA: WH Wolfe.

———. 1993. *Unhallowed Intrusion: A History of Cherokee Families in Forsyth County, Georgia.* Alpharetta, GA: W. H. Wolfe.

Tyner, James W. 1974. *Those Who Cried: The 16,000: A Record of the Individual Cherokees Listed in the United States Office Census of the Cherokee Nation Conducted in 1835.* Norman, OK: Chi-ga-u.

USGenWeb Census Project. 2012. "Cherokee Native Americans of the Five Civilized Tribes." http://www.us-census.org/native/cherokee/index.html.

Warren, Mary Bondurant, and Eve B. Weeks. 1987. *Whites among the Cherokees: Georgia 1828–1838.* Danielsville, GA: Heritage Papers.

Wikipedia. 2017. "Cherokee Freedmen." https://en.wikipedia.org/wiki/Cherokee#Cherokee_Freedmen. https://en.wikipedia.org/wiki/Muscogee_people

*Please view my "public" Family Tree on Ancestry.com
*Please view all my videos on YouTube by searching: Eagle Eye Banks 2017

CPSIA information can be obtained
at www.ICGtesting.com
Printed in the USA
LVHW07n0358010818
585568LV00009B/77/P